THE EVIDENCE:

Three minutes after Thomas Alva Edison died, four clocks in his lab stopped working.

James Chaffin's father appeared to him in a dream and revealed the location of an unsuspected will which was later upheld by the courts.

The day Taylor Caldwell's husband was buried her resurrection lily shrub bloomed for the first time in twenty-one years.

THE CONCLUSION:

THE CASE FOR IMMORTALITY offers convincing proof from mediums, cases of apparitions, temporary death, memories of previous lives, and material manifestations that there is some form of existence after death.

"Here is a major contribution to paraphysical phenomena, a book that will be read, discussed, and studied for years to come."
—THE PITTSBURGH PRESS

SIGNET Books of Special Interest

The Case
for
Immortality

by
ALLEN SPRAGGETT

A SIGNET BOOK

NEW AMERICAN LIBRARY

TIMES MIRROR

For My Friend
William V. Rauscher,

Who Lives His Belief That
Man's Spirit Transcends Death

Library of Congress Catalog Card Number: 73-91365

This is a reprint of a hardcover edition published by The New American Library, Inc., and distributed by W. W. Norton & Company, Inc. The hardcover edition was published simultaneously in Canada by George McLeod, Ltd., Toronto.

SIGNET, SIGNET CLASSICS, MENTOR, PLUME AND MERIDIAN BOOKS are published by The New American Library, Inc., 1301 Avenue of the Americas, New York, New York 10019

First Printing, March, 1975

1 2 3 4 5 6 7 8 9

PRINTED IN THE UNITED STATES OF AMERICA

Contents

A Slight Case of Dying

In 1970 Leslie Sharpe, a 68-year-old retired railway employee in Toronto, temporarily died.

His first-hand account of what it's like to die appeared in the May 1971 issue of the journal of the Canadian Medical Association. Drs. R. L. MacMillan and K. W. G. Brown, codirectors of the coronary care unit at Toronto General Hospital, said that Mr. Sharpe's account "could be the experience of the soul leaving the body."

Leslie Sharpe was taken to the hospital after his family physician diagnosed a pain in his left arm as a heart attack. The next morning the patient was glancing at his watch while hooked up to an electrocardiograph monitoring his heart activity when suddenly—well, let him tell it.

"I gave a very, very deep sigh," he recalled, "and my head flopped over to the right. I thought, why did my head flop over? I didn't move it.

"Then suddenly I am looking at my own body from the waist up, face to face as though in a mirror in which I appear to be in the lower left corner. Almost immediately I saw myself leaving my body, coming out through my head and shoulders. I did not see my lower limbs.

"The body leaving me was not exactly in vapor form, yet it seemed to expand very slightly once it was clear of me.

"Suddenly I am sitting on a very small object traveling at great speed, out and up into a dull blue-gray sky at a 45-degree angle.

"Down below me, to my left, I saw a pure white cloud-like substance also moving up on a line that would intersect my course. It was perfectly rectangular in shape but full of holes like a sponge.

"My next sensation was of floating in a bright, pale yellow light—a very delightful feeling.

"I continued to float, enjoying the most beautiful, tranquil sensation.

"Then there were sledge-hammer blows to my left side. They created no actual pain but jarred me so much I had difficulty in retaining my balance. I began to count then and when I got to six I said aloud: 'What the hell are you doing to me?' and opened my eyes."

At this point, said Mr. Sharpe, he recognized doctors and nurses around his bed who told him he had suffered a cardiac arrest and had just received a series of six electric shocks to start his heart beating again.

He had been clinically dead, and now he was alive.

CHAPTER 1

Is Life After Death Possible?

You will never die.

A statement of faith? Yet, but in this book I hope to show that it is a faith based on fact.

The statement, to be sure, needs a little interpretation.

It does not mean, of course, that you will never experience what men call death. I'm not suggesting that science has discovered, or is about to discover, a way of bypassing death.

It *does* mean that something which is identifiably "you" will survive death.

Your brain, someday, will flicker out, your heart shut down, your vital processes be reduced to absolute zero. But *you*—that inner self which can inspect your own brain waves, learn to control the rate of your heartbeat, and suffer the loss of an arm or leg without being diminished —that *you* will outlive your physical body.

Where, you ask, is the evidence? That is precisely what I want you now to consider.

Fashions change in ideas as in clothes, and today it is unfashionable, in educated circles at least and particularly among biologists, to credit the notion of a life after death.

To start with, that school of philosophers called linguistic analysts argues that the very phrase "life after death" is an absurd contradiction in terms—like "married bachelor" or "square circle." How, ask these radical skeptics, can one seriously consider a concept which cannot even be expressed in meaningful language?

As for the biologists—well, though few would care to put it as crudely as the eighteenth-century Frenchman, Cabanis, who said that "the brain secretes thought as the liver secretes bile," no doubt most would agree with the tenor of that statement.

Mind and brain, says current dogma, are virtually identical, two sides of the same phenomenon. Consciousness, in this view, can no more be separated from the brain which gives rise to it than can the glow around the electric light from the bulb. When the bulb is switched off, the light goes out. And when the human brain dies, the spark of consciousness it nourished fades back into that inky void of unknowing from which, say the skeptics somberly, all things come and to which all things ultimately will return.

Another objection to the idea of life after death is the alleged unimaginability of any plausible form which such existence could take.

Since the inhabitants of the next world have left their bodies behind, runs this argument, are they, then, mere oblong blurs, blobs of nothingness? If they possess no physical dimensions, and therefore occupy no space, the world they inhabit must have neither dimensions nor location; in which case, it is situated precisely nowhere.

How, though, can a world exist without a location?

If, on the other hand, the dead do have bodies of some sort—"subtle" or "astral" bodies, let us say—then these must take up room and the world they inhabit must have a location in space, just as Cleveland has, or London, or Timbuctu. But if so, where *is* this next world? Straight up, as tradition suggests? How far? Could it, for example, be reached by a space ship?

The problem, argue the skeptics, is that any kind of after-death existence, whether with or without bodies, boggles the imagination and is, quite literally, inconceivable.

Another argument against life after death hinges on the question of what exactly it is in man which could plausibly survive. The brain dies. The heart dies. The whole body dies, shrivels, and decays. What, then, is left?

Science, we are told, knows nothing about a nonphysical entity which would be deathproof. All that science knows are material entities. Even moonshine has weight and is, therefore, in the broadest sense of the word, material—that is to say, it can be measured and is subject to time and space relationships.

How are we to imagine a "soul" or "spirit" having neither shape, size, nor other measurable properties? Obviously, says the argument, such an amorphous thing is a chimera—something which cannot exist in the real world.

Moreover, continues this argument, how *could* you survive without your physical body—allowing, for the moment, that such survival is conceivable—when that body is an integral part of you; indeed, in a real sense, *is* you. Consider, for argument's sake, that if you were transplanted into a totally different body—say, that of a squid, or a duck-billed platypus—you would no longer be you. You would become somebody, or something, else. The particular physical body which is yours and the environment with which it interacts are an absolutely essential part of you-ness. Then even if something lived on after the destruction of your body, that bodiless cipher, whatever it might be, would not be you.

Finally, there is the psychological argument against the concept of life after death.

This, simply put, says that belief in survival is merely a manifestation of the will to believe. In evidence, consider that few people, if any, carry the idea to its logical conclusion. If a human being survives death, why not, as Voltaire suggested, a flea? If one objects to conferring an immortal soul on so lowly a creature, what about a cat or a dog? They think, after a fashion, and certainly they experience emotions. But when the family poodle dies does anybody, besides a few eccentric pet worshipers, really believe that dear departed Fido has gone to some great kennel in the sky?

These, as I see them, are the main arguments brought against the concept of life after death. They could be summed up: The concept is plainly contrary to common sense.

My reply is, first, that in matters of ultimate reality common sense is always wrong. (Spraggett's Law says, more formally, that the truth of anything is in inverse ratio to the square of its plausibility.)

This point is worth pursuing because if we are to examine the evidence for an after-life honestly and dispassionately we must free ourselves from the tyranny of common sense. Admittedly, any discussion of a next world is bound to strike a certain type of rationalist as being straight out of *Alice in Wonderland*. Familiar concepts are stood on their heads, and things which are impossible become routine. But much the same phenomenon occurs in the laboratory of a nuclear physicist.

The electron theory of matter, for example, is based on something other than common sense. The notion that physical objects are composed of points of energy in a particular pattern or configuration, and that these have neither taste, smell, visible form, or tangibility—such things being *sense data* contributed by our minds, so that the whole universe of matter is reduced to the mind's interpretation of electrical excitement in the cerebral cortex—this, I say, is utterly contrary to common sense.

But common sense does not properly belong in a world where, as Sir Arthur Eddington observed, a table "is mostly emptiness, and sparsely scattered in that emptiness are numerous electric charges rushing about with great speed; but their combined bulk amounts to less than a billionth of the bulk of the table itself." [1]

When the electron theory of matter gave birth to the explosion at Alamagordo, New Mexico, on July 16, 1945, which ushered in the Atomic Age, it also vaporized the claims of common sense as an arbiter of what is or is not possible in this vast, mysterious, paradoxical universe.

(To drive, hopefully, the final nail into the coffin of common sense, consider that for theoretical physicists the question is not whether an idea is too crazy to be true, but, as nuclear pioneer Niels Bohr once remarked, whether it is crazy *enough* to be true. "For any speculation which does not at first glance look crazy," agreed physicist Freeman Dyson, "there is no hope." [2])

On the face of it, the most telling argument against survival after death is that which equates mind with brain.

[1] Arthur Eddington, *The Nature of the Physical World* (New York, Macmillan Company, 1929).
[2] Freeman Dyson, *Scientific American* (September, 1959).

The view that consciousness, or mental states, depend on the brain and necessarily end with brain-death seems almost self-evident, resting as it does on some common observations.

For example, we all know that when the higher brain centers are temporarily out of action due to a blow on the head, or drugs, unconsciousness is the result. And we also know that damage to the brain impairs mental function, the nature and extent of that impairment depending on the location and extent of the damage.

Thus, a lesion in a particular part of the brain is followed by amnesia for recent events, let us say, while the same lesion at a different site is followed by speech difficulties (such as aphasia, the inability to put words in meaningful sequence), or the loss of the capacity to recognize anybody, even one's own wife. If the brain damage is massive, as after a stroke, there is a correspondingly gross impairment of mental function.

Such observations certainly suggest that the mind depends entirely on the brain and, therefore, could not possibly outlive it—any more than the image on the television screen could outlast the picture tube.

Let us, however, look more deeply into this intimate duality of mind and brain.

Does consciousness *really* cease when the cerebral cortex—that part of the brain reputed to govern consciousness—is temporarily not functioning, as, for example, during a period of general anesthesia? The answer, contrary to appearances, is no. Consider the evidence.

More and more doctors are becoming aware that the totally anesthetized patient on the operating table hears everything that goes on. Though these perceptions rarely seep through to conscious awareness, they lodge in the patient's deep mind and, under certain conditions, can be recalled. Even if not consciously remembered, such perceptions can influence the patient's mental state. Accordingly, surgeons are cautioned not to make negative remarks about the patient's condition. "Unconscious," we are learning, does not necessarily mean "unaware."

Psychologist Leslie LeCron, one of America's foremost authorities on hypnosis, recounts how a 30-year-old man's marked inferiority feelings, which stemmed from an irrational conviction that he was illegitimate, were traced to remarks he overheard during a tonsillectomy 12 years before.

While hypnotized, the patient, who had been under general anesthesia for the operation, remembered hearing his father, a physician, say, "You're just a bastard, a little bastard," which his unconscious mind interpreted literally (as the unconscious, sometimes exasperatingly, is wont to do). However, in the hypnotic state he realized, for the first time, that the remark had not been directed at him at all but was spoken, as affectionate banter, to another doctor who was present.[3]

The significant point for us in this incident is that the young man, though anesthetized ("unconscious"), had been able to perceive and register verbal stimuli. The part of his brain which governs consciousness was temporarily disconnected, switched off, yet evidently perception, an attribute of consciousness, continued. How?

No less an authority than the great psychiatrist, Dr. C. G. Jung, alluded to similar experiences which, on the assumption that the mind is totally dependent on the brain, appear to be inexplicable.

[3] Leslie LeCron, *Self Hypnotism* (Englewood Cliffs, New Jersey, Prentice-Hall, 1964).

Jung speaks of "certain astonishing observations" in cases of profound syncope (fainting) after acute injuries to the brain and in severe states of collapse.

> In both situations, total loss of consciousness can be accompanied by perceptions of the outside world and vivid dream experiences. Since the cerebral cortex, the seat of consciousness, is not functioning at these times, there is as yet no explanation for such phenomena.[4]

These phenomena point to the conclusion that the mind, while it expresses itself through the brain, is not wholly, nor necessarily, dependent on it. At times, it seems, perceptions can bypass the brain and reach the mind directly.

Suggestive of the same conclusion are certain experiments by the distinguished neurologist, Wilder Penfield. Describing how electrical stimulation of different parts of the human brain triggers different reactions in a subject, Penfield reports:

> If the electrode is applied to one of the speech areas of the dominant hemisphere . . . the patient is silent. . . . He can no longer find words to express his thoughts. But they come with a rush when the electrode is lifted and he says, then, the things he was trying to say while the electrode was interfering with his employment of the speech area of the cortex.[5]

Note the language the neurologist uses. The "he" which refers to the patient appears to be separate, or certainly

[4] C. G. Jung, *Memories, Dreams, Reflections* (New York, New York Books, 1963).

[5] Hornell Hart, *The Enigma of Survival* (Springfield, Illinois, Charles C. Thomas Publisher, 1959).

distinguishable, from the brain. By stimulating part of the patient's cortex Penfield deprived "him" of words to express "his" thoughts. But who is this "he" who can be gagged by tinkering with his brain? Surely the pronoun does not refer merely to another part of the brain. If that were so, this would be a case of one part of the brain saying to a different part: "Let me express my thoughts, let me have words."

A more likely interpretation—and the one to which Penfield himself appears to incline—is that behind or within the brain, using it as an operator uses a computer, lurks the thinker himself.

Curious evidence that mind and brain, though intimately related, are quite different also comes from the study of Siamese twins. These are monozygotic, or uniovular, twins—that is to say, two bodies and brains developed from a single fertilized cell and therefore genetically identical—who, by reason of being physically conjoined, share an identical environment. Now if human personality is *wholly* the product of the brain and body, plus environmental influences, Siamese twins, sharing as they do identical brains, bodies, and environments, should have identical personalities. They should be psychological carbon-copies. But are they?

Evidently not. A British psychiatrist, Dr. H. Tudor Edmunds, cites the case of Siamese twins, Mary and Margaret, joined through a long lifetime at the base of the spine, who had totally dissimilar personalities.

> Mary [said Dr. Edmunds] was easy going and carefree, while Margaret was highly strung and always worried about health and financial matters. . . . Here is a case of sustained identical environment of a most intimate

and complete nature over a considerable period of years. Yet the identical brains and environment were unable to prevent two very different personalities from developing.[6]

This pronounced disparity between the personalities of two genetic duplicates who experienced the same life-long environment strongly suggests that human personality has a more than biological—or better, a more than physiological—basis. There must be a nonphysical component.

A crude analogy to the mind-brain-body relationship is the relationship in which a virtuoso stands to his violin. Consider that the virtuoso's performance, regardless of his musical skill, depends in large measure on his instrument. If a string breaks, the performance suffers; if all the strings break—well, any further violin playing by the virtuoso must be in his imagination only. Yet whatever happens to his instrument the violinist remains whole.

So the invisible thinker may use his brain as an instrument of self-expression. Damage to the instrument, though it does not impair the thinker, inhibits his ability to express himself. And when, at death, the instrument is destroyed, the thinker's continued expression on the physical plane is impossible. But does the thinker therefore cease to exist? That does not follow in logic at all.

Speaking of "logic," that word before which some philosophers prostrate themselves, the argument that life after death is ruled out because the phrase itself is a meaningless contradiction in terms strikes me as being a mere semantic quibble.

The phrase "life after death," I submit, is not an absurdity but a paradox. And a paradox can be true.

[6] H. Tudor Edmunds, "Mind Is Not Produced by the Brain," *Two Worlds* (London, 1968).

Consider, for example, the paradox which in physics is known as the Principle of Complementarity. It says that light is composed of both waves and discrete particles (called quanta or photons)—a state of affairs which is manifestly illogical. Light surely must be either waves *or* particles; it cannot be both. But apparently it is. (A wit reconciled the contradiction by saying it was composed of "waveicles.") The paradox is that light sometimes behaves as though it were a wave phenomenon, and at other times as though it were composed of separate particles. Nature, being a woman, disdains logic.

Similarly, the argument that life after death is inconceivable ignores the fact that the queer, shadowy entities of subatomic physics are equally inconceivable.

Actually, the correct word is not inconceivable but unvisualizable. We can conceive of, but we cannot *visualize*, a next world. But then neither can we visualize that basic building block of matter, the electron, which, as Sir James Jeans once remarked, does not have a definite position in space and takes up no more room than "a fear, an anxiety or an uncertainty." [7]

If our minds cannot visualize the fundamental stuff of the physical world, should we wonder that we have difficulty visualizing the next world?

There are, in fact, a number of hypotheses about the form the next world could take which consider precisely such issues as whether that world has dimensions and location, and, if so, where. These hypotheses will be explored in later chapters.

What about the argument which says that there is not, and indeed cannot be, anything in man which could plausibly survive the death of the physical body?

[7] Lincoln Barnett, *The Universe and Dr. Einstein* (New York, Harper & Row, 1948).

To answer this objection we must return to the question of the distinction between brain and consciousness, although approaching it this time from a somewhat different angle.

Some scientists say that consciousness—or thoughts, mental states, whatever you wish to call the phenomenon of I-ness—are patterns of electrical activity in the brain. But are these electrical discharges really thinking itself or merely the physical concomitants of thinking?

Surely, ideas in the mind are *not* the same thing as electrical charges in the brain. Even a thoroughgoing materialist has agreed that ideas cannot be equated with physical entities but are, rather, "non-material meanings expressing the relations between objects and events." [8] Though the passage of an idea through the mind may be the occasion of characteristic electrical activity in the brain, the two are manifestly not identical. One might as well argue that because fear causes an elevation in blood pressure, fear *is* an elevation in blood pressure.

The radical question is: Are the criteria of matter—namely, measurability and being subject to time and space relationships—applicable to ideas in the mind?

Well, it makes no sense to ask how much room an idea takes up, or whether the idea of a mouse is smaller than the idea of an elephant, or whether the idea of yesterday comes before the idea of today. Categories of time and space do not apply in the realm of ideas.

When a person says he has a place for you in his thoughts, where is such a place? It would be impossible to chart its latitude and longitude but it is nonetheless real for that.

[8] Corliss Lamont, *The Illusion of Immortality* (New York, Philosophical Library, 1953).

Whatever it is in man that spins ideas, and therefore operates even now in a world beyond time and space, there is no reason why such a thing should perish at death. Being timeless and spaceless, it may well be deathless.

The psychological argument against life after death, which says that the concept is sheer wish fulfillment, is naïve.

For one thing, the fact that we may want something to be true does not necessarily prove that it isn't true. Most people would want art and romance to exist if they didn't, but they do.

Moreover, the argument assumes that everybody, or nearly everybody, wants to survive death. That is far from obvious. Taylor Caldwell, the novelist, no doubt speaks for others besides herself when she calls life "a monstrous, painful, agonizing affair," and, in spite of her own numerous psychic experiences, rejects the possibility of survival —because, admittedly, she wants to.[9]

Which leads to another point: The will to believe has an antithesis in the will not to believe. I have encountered both, and one can be just as powerful as the other. If there are people who would crucify reason to believe in life after death, there are others, I'm persuaded, who would refuse to believe even if their own deceased mothers materialized on prime-time television with a dozen scientists in attendance.

The issue of whether man does or does not survive death must be considered not on the basis of emotion but of reason, of the *evidence*. We have weighed the main arguments against an after-life and found them wanting. Now let us examine the positive empirical

[9] Taylor Caldwell, *Ladies Home Journal* (October, 1972).

evidence which has convinced many thoughtful, perceptive people that man is inherently impervious to death.

The evidence comes, in the first place, from experiences usually classified as extrasensory perception, or ESP. Such phenomena are not in the least "supernatural"—a word that is obsolete. As part of nature, they are perfectly natural; but since they are above or outside the normal course of human experiences they qualify for the adjective *supernormal*.

From the study of ESP we discover that the human psyche, here and now, transcends time and space. One mind can touch another, independently of the physical senses and of distance (this is called *telepathy*); or the mind can perceive distant events, or pick up "memories" from physical objects (*clairvoyance*); or project itself into the future (*precognition*); or directly influence physical objects (*psychokinesis*).

There is also evidence that certain people with unusual psychic gifts, called mediums, can at times produce information which appears to come from deceased human beings.

There is evidence that some persons who have clinically died and been revived have experienced a preview of the after-death state.

There is evidence, too, that some people remember having died several times and being reborn in successive physical embodiments.

Let us now take a close look at these fascinating signs which point to the conclusion that you will never die.

CHAPTER 2

The Evidence from Mediumship

A medium is an individual of unusual psychic ability who, in the spiritualist view, acts as a transmitter between worlds.

A medium is a human telephone, so to speak, through which people on this side of the experience called death purportedly can communicate with those on the other side.

Usually a medium functions while in a trance—a kind of waking sleep in which the conscious, reasoning mind recedes and the unconscious, where psychic abilities reside, comes to the fore.

In a trance, the medium purports to be taken over by a "control" or "spirit guide"—the alleged discarnate personality who regularly manifests through a particular medium and serves as a go-between for other spirits wishing to communicate. Less frequently the medium may be controlled by a communicator whom the sitter knew in life.

In the first instance the medium's control passes on to the sitter messages purporting to come from his dead friends or loved ones, as a telephone operator, during a long-distance call with a poor connection, might pass messages back and forth between the two parties. In the second instance, when the medium appears to be taken over by the communicating spirit, the messages are given to the sitter directly, and he may recognize personal characteristics of his deceased friend or a person whom he loved.

The late C. J. Ducasse, one-time head of the department of philosophy at Brown University, and a convinced survivalist, suggested an analogue of these two types of communication through a medium.

> Let us suppose . . . that a friend of ours, Joe Doe, had been aboard an airplane which has crashed in the ocean, and that no survivors have been found; but that, some time later, our telephone rings and (a) that a voice we recognize as John Doe's is heard and a conversation with it held which convinces us that the speaker is really John Doe. Or alternately, let us suppose (b) that the voice heard is not John Doe's but that of some other person seemingly relaying his words to us and ours to him; and that the conversation so held does convince us that the person with whom we are conversing through that intermediary is John Doe.[1]

The criterion for evaluating a mediumistic communication, said Ducasse, is precisely the same as for evaluating the hypothetical phone call from the missing friend, namely, can the person on the other end of the line establish his identity beyond a reasonable doubt?

How would one go about establishing that identity?

Well, we would expect our friend, if it were he, to be familiar with certain facts—his wife's name, the name of the family cat, what his own mother called him when he was a child, obscure incidents from his life. Interestingly,

[1] C. J. Ducasse, "What Would Constitute Conclusive Evidence of Survival After Death?" *Journal of the American Society for Psychical Research,* Vol. 41 (December, 1962).

the more trivial the fact, the more evidential. Though people other than John Doe might know his wife's name, and even the name of the family cat, it is unlikely that any would know the affectionate name his mother called him as a child.

Probably we would ply the caller with test questions of our own: Where did we stay in London when we were there together on such-and-such a date? Or, what was the title of the book you gave me on my twenty-first birthday?

In the best cases of purported communication with the dead, these are just the sort of data which emerge.

Consider a well-attested case involving the great eighteenth-century scientist and seer, Emanuel Swedenborg. A versatile genius, called "the northern Plato" by Kant, and by Carlyle "one of the three or four greatest intellects which have appeared upon the planet," Swedenborg devoted himself to science until he was middle-aged, then had a series of tremendous mystical experiences which led to a powerful form of mediumship. He claimed to be caught up into the next world and to converse with the spirits of the dead. This particular case, typical of those that made Swedenborg famous, was first reported by Count Höpken, a Swedish noble.

> Swedenborg was one day at a court reception. Her Majesty [Louisa Ulrica, Queen of Sweden, formerly a Prussian princess] asked him about different things in the other life, and lastly whether he had seen, or talked with, her brother, the Prince Royal of Prussia. He answered no. Her Majesty then requested Swedenborg to ask after him and to give him her greeting. . . . At the next reception Swedenborg again appeared at court; and while the Queen was in the so-called white room, sur-

rounded by her ladies of honor, he came boldly in. . . . Swedenborg not only greeted the Queen from her brother but also gave her brother's apologies for not having answered her last letter. The brother wished to do so now through Swedenborg, which he accordingly did. The Queen was greatly overcome and said, "No one, except God, knows this secret." [2]

Another, even more remarkable, case in which Swedenborg acted as a medium concerned the widow of the Dutch ambassador to Stockholm, Madame Marteville, and a missing receipt.

The widow was troubled when a goldsmith named Croon presented her with a bill for a silver tea service which her late husband had purchased. She was certain that her husband must have paid the bill but she could not find the receipt.

Since the amount involved was substantial, the ambassador's widow sought help from the celebrated Baron Swedenborg (he was a member of the Swedish nobility). If, as people claimed, he had the ability to communicate with departed spirits, would he be good enough to ask her husband about the debt? Swedenborg promised that he would.

Three days later he called at the widow's house. After a moment for the social courtesies, Madame Marteville blurted out: "Tell me, were you able to reach my husband?"

"Indeed," replied Swedenborg in his cool way. "As you surmised the debt was paid, seven months before his death. Your husband told me that you will find the receipt in a secret compartment in his desk."

---

[2] George Trobridge *Swedenborg: Life and Teaching* (New York, Swedenborg Foundation, Inc., 1962).

In the presence of witnesses, the ambassador's widow, following Swedenborg's directions, looked for a hidden compartment situated just beneath the left-hand drawer in her husband's desk. She found it precisely where Swedenborg said it was—though she had known nothing of its existence, much less its location—and inside was the missing receipt.[3]

These two cases appear to meet the criteria suggested by Ducasse. In each the information seems convincingly to have come from the alleged deceased communicator. The Queen of Sweden avowed that the secret Swedenborg mentioned was known only to her and her deceased brother (and, as she expressed it, to God). The location of the missing receipt was known to no living person, making its discovery even more striking as evidence of discarnate intervention.

A recent case, similar to these in some respects, was reported by the Pulitzer Prize-winning novelist and social crusader, Upton Sinclair.

Sinclair's second wife, Mary, died in 1961 at the age of 70. A few days later Sinclair received a letter from a stranger in another state (he himself lived in California) saying that in a séance with the noted medium, Arthur Ford, a communication had been received from someone who identified herself as Mary Craig Sinclair. (The novelist and his wife had known Ford some 30 years before but had had no contact with him in the intervening period.) As evidence that it *was* she, the communicator asked that her husband be told that three "fainting spells" she suffered shortly before her death, which in each instance had resulted in a bad fall, were actually light strokes.

[3] Trobridge, *Swedenborg: Life and Teaching.*

Upton Sinclair called the doctor who, with two other physicians, had performed an autopsy on his wife's body. Without any inkling of why he was being asked, the doctor confirmed that brain lesions indicated that Mrs. Sinclair had suffered three light strokes.[4]

As evidence for discarnate intervention this case is peculiarly impressive. The information communicated was known only to the deceased person and the doctors who performed the autopsy. Even her husband, who received the message, though aware of his wife's "fainting spells," had no idea of their true cause. It would seem, then, that the information could only have come from one source—the surviving mind of Mary Craig Sinclair.

To be sure, we should note here that other hypotheses besides the survival one have been advanced to explain cases such as these mentioned, and we will consider the counterhypotheses later in this chapter. But first, let us examine some further examples of purported messages from the dead.

Another striking case involving Arthur Ford was reported by Dr. Amos Horlacher, a Protestant clergyman who at one time was dean of men at Pennsylvania's Dickinson College.

In May of 1938 Dr. Horlacher, on the spur of the moment, attended a psychic demonstration held by Ford in New York's Roosevelt Hotel. On this occasion the medium did not go into a trance but simply stood up before the audience of several hundred people, breathed deeply a few times to put himself into a "hypnoidal" state (as he called it), and then passed on messages which he said he could hear the dead speaking to him. (Ford's special

---

[4] Upton Sinclair, *Mental Radio* (New York, Collier Books, 1971).

gift was "clairaudience," the auditory counterpart of clairvoyance.)

Dr. Horlacher concentrated on the name of a man, Arthur J. Beyfield, who had been his close friend at Williamsport-Dickinson Seminary in the years from 1920 to 1923 and who had been dead for six or seven years. He was the one person Horlacher had known very well who was dead; and, thought the clergyman, "if there is any reality in this psychic business he's the one who will communicate with me."

No message came from Arthur Beyfield, however, though a number of people in the audience acknowledged that communications directed to them were remarkably evidential. Then, suddenly, Arthur Ford, who had finished his demonstration and sat down, stood up again.

"Before we close the meeting," he said, "I would like to say that I hear a strange message.

"I seem to get the words 'The Three Musketeers.' Now I get some initials—A.J.B. Is there anyone in this audience who would recognize or have any connection with anything I have said? Certainly I do not."

Amos Horlacher was jolted by Ford's remarks, recognizing them immediately as being connected with his deceased friend, Arthur J. Beyfield. But before he could speak the medium continued.

> I have something more. This voice reveals that the person who is being sought is in this audience. He is further to be found as a young man, that is to say, a man short of 40 years, who is a clergyman in one of our Evangelical churches.
>
> The further message I have is that A.J.B. wants him to know that he is happy where he is, that he does not get any spots and does not have to walk them off on

Saturday morning. And that person whom he is addressing would instantly understand the meaning of what he
is saying.

Dr. Horlacher did indeed understand the message.

The reference to "spots" which the communicator had
had "to walk off on Saturday morning" reminded Horlacher of the unpopular demerit system at the seminary
he and Beyfield had attended. The demerits, awarded
for various student misdemeanors, were called "spots"
and could be removed only by the offender's performing
a prescribed number of military drill exercises in the
college gymnasium on Saturday mornings.[5]

Applying Ducasse's analogy of the phone call from a
missing friend, this message contained enough evidence
of having indeed come from the person who purported
to be communicating to impress even the die-hard skeptic.
(I do not say "convince," but "impress.")

In fact, if Arthur Beyfield had been missing, rather
than known to be dead, such a message probably would
have inspired belief that he was still alive. The fact that
Beyfield *was* dead and not simply missing does not, however, dilute the force of the evidence.

If somebody objects, "But surely there *is* a big difference since we know that missing persons sometimes turn
up alive whereas the dead never do," I would point out
that this is prejudging the case. The question of whether
the dead *are* alive and able to communicate is precisely
what is at issue; one cannot fairly argue against the
evidence on the premise that such communication never
happens when it is the evidence which alone can settle
that question.

[5] Alison J. Smith, *Immortality: The Scientific Evidence* (Englewood Cliffs, New Jersey, Prentice-Hall, 1954).

THE CASE FOR IMMORTALITY

The information produced by the medium was, I submit, just the sort of evidential trivia which old school chums, chancing to meet after many years, would be likely to recall. If these recollections did not proceed from the mind of the dead Arthur Beyfield, from whence did they come?

Sometimes—and this can be peculiarly convincing—a message through one medium is confirmed by another message received independently through a second medium.

Such a case of "cross communication," suggesting an objective pattern of events observed by discarnates rather than one woven by the minds of the mediums themselves, is reported by the Reverend Canon William V. Rauscher, rector of Christ Episcopal Church, Woodbury, New Jersey.

The first message here came during a séance held with Olga Worrall, a noted Baltimore medium and spiritual healer. This took place in Philadelphia on August 24, 1968. Present, besides Canon Rauscher, was his friend, another Episcopal priest, the Reverend (now Canon) Robert Lewis.

"Bob," said the medium, addressing Father Lewis, "there is a Father John present. He is standing right by you. . . . Do you know a Father John?"

"Yes, Olga, that has meaning to me," Lewis acknowledged. He was thinking of a Father John, now deceased, who had once been vicar of All Saints Episcopal Church in Hershey, Pennsylvania.

"He says," continued the medium, "that you don't have your own church, or you are not in charge. But you are going to have your own church very soon."

Unknown to the medium, the Reverend Gerald Minchin, rector of St. Mary's Episcopal Church in Haddon

Heights, New Jersey, the parish where Robert Lewis served as curate, had come to him four days earlier and revealed his decision to retire in December. At this point nobody besides Father Lewis, not even the bishop, knew of Canon Minchin's retirement plans.

"Now they are placing a church right down over your head," Olga Worrall said to Lewis.

After the séance, the two clergymen asked the three other people present to keep the message confidential, at least for the time being, which all agreed to do.

Six days later the senior warden of St. Mary's Church came to Robert Lewis and said he had been informed by the rector of his planned retirement. He pledged his support to Lewis as a candidate for rector of the 1,300-member parish.

Curious about whether another medium would confirm Olga Worrall's prediction, Lewis and Rauscher arranged a sitting with Arthur Ford on September 17.

The medium's control, "Fletcher" (who claimed to be a French-Canadian Ford had known as a child), said to Father Lewis: "Several spirits are here. One man I have not seen before—Duncan. He says he is happy to be here, and that you are causing quite a bit of excitement and speculation."

Lewis recognized this as the Reverend James M. Duncan, a priest with whom he once worked as a curate in Washington, D.C., and at whose funeral he had taken part.

Fletcher said that Duncan spoke about a big change coming for Lewis—an "elevation." It was "a moving up not a moving away."

Then another purported spirit broke in with: "I greet the new rector."

On September 23, less than a week after this séance, Robert Lewis was elected rector of St. Mary's Church by a unanimous vote of the vestry, and his name also was at the top of the list of candidates submitted by the bishop.[6]

In this case two mediums independently produced messages which dovetailed and which, considering that the alleged communicators were priests who had known Father Lewis well, were perfectly in character.

Sometimes the communicator, purportedly speaking through an entranced medium, succeeds in projecting a remarkably vivid and lifelike impression of himself as the sitter remembers him.

Professor C. D. Broad, a seasoned and critical researcher, commented on this phenomenon in the mediumship of Britain's celebrated Mrs. Gladys Osborne Leonard.

> With some sitters, after they have had a good many sittings, there happens a . . . development of a very startling kind. The voice and mannerisms change completely, e.g., a gruff male voice or a typical clergyman's voice may issue from the medium's lips. . . . It is as if a certain deceased person, e.g., John, or Etta, were using the body to speak with. It is alleged by the sitters that the intonations, verbal mannerisms, etc., of the ostensible communicator are often reproduced with startling exactness, although Mrs. Leonard has never met the individual in life.[7]

In the mediumship of the extraordinary Boston medium, Mrs. Lenore Piper—the woman who convinced William James, greatest of American psychologists, of the

[6] William V. Rauscher, "A Case of Cross-Communication," *Spiritual Frontiers*, Vol. 1 (Winter, 1969).
[7] Hart, *The Enigma of Survival*.

reality of supernormal phenomena—this kind of control by the communicator was so complete that often long, detailed conversations took place between the communicator and the sitter. These included the normal give-and-take of conversation between two living persons. This quality of seemingly absolute naturalness and spontaneity was particularly evident in communications from one "George Pelham" (a pseudonym for Pellew, a young lawyer who died in 1892) to friends and members of his family.[8]

Out of at least 150 people who had sittings with Mrs. Piper after the George Pelham personality first manifested, this communicator correctly recognized 30 as former friends of his. These recognitions were spontaneous, the sitters having been told beforehand not to provide any clues. There was no case of false recognition (that is to say, where Pelham greeted as a friend someone whom in fact he had never known). And there was only one case in which he failed to recognize a person he *had* known—and this was understandable inasmuch as it was a young woman he had known only as a child some nine years before.

Do the cases we have cited establish, as an indisputable reality, communication with the dead?

Before we could even consider saying that, we must examine the antisurvivalist counterhypotheses. There are only two, really. The first is that the medium acquired the evidential information by normal means, probably fraud.

Could the medium, in these cases, have used normal

[8] C. J. Ducasse, *The Belief in a Life After Death* (Springfield, Illinois, Charles C. Thomas Publisher, 1961).

means, whether innocent or culpable, to discover those facts ostensibly communicated by the dead?

The question must be taken very seriously. Besides the possibility of the medium having innocently picked up the information—by reading, conversation, or some other way—the history of spiritualism reveals only too clearly that many mediums have used trickery. Even genuine mediums have been known to lapse into fraud.

However, in the cases under consideration normal acquisition of the information seems extremely—one might even say, infinitely—unlikely.

Consider again the two incidents involving Emanuel Swedenborg. It is improbable, to say the least, that he should have been privy to a secret between the Queen of Sweden and her deceased brother; or that he could have surmised in any normal way the whereabouts of the receipt hidden by the Dutch ambassador.

In the two cases involving Arthur Ford, normal sources of information seem similarly precluded.

Only the doctors knew that Upton Sinclair's wife had suffered three light strokes; and in the case of Amos Holacher, who received the evidential message from his dead college chum, the discovery of this information through prior research by the medium, though theoretically possible, is ruled out by Ford's not knowing that the clergyman would be present.

In the case in which the two mediums, Olga Worrall and Arthur Ford, independently predicted that the Reverend Robert Lewis was to become a rector, there is no evidence of collusion by these mediums, though admittedly it was possible. Moreover, even if Mrs. Worrall had mentioned her prediction to Ford, this would not explain how *she* came to make it when, at the time, the incumbent rector's decision to retire was known only to Father Lewis. (For that matter, this decision did not necessarily mean that Lewis, as curate, would automatically step into the rector's shoes.)

The second counterhypothesis to survival is super-ESP in the medium; in other words, the information came not from the dead, as alleged, but from the medium's own psychic powers.

The fact that a medium honestly thinks the information is from departed spirits does not guarantee for a moment that it is. Mediums sometimes give out information which they believe to be true, and which they interpret as proceeding from a discarnate communicator, but which turns out to be false.

The dilemma is this: Any verifiable information which comes through a medium, purportedly from the dead, is either (a) known to some living person and therefore accessible to *telepathy;* (b) contained in a document somewhere, and therefore accessible to *clairvoyance;* or, (c) lies in the future and is accessible to *precognition.* All these extrasensory abilities are known to be practiced by living people; therefore, says the antisurvivalist, there is no reason to postulate communication by the dead.

Even mediums who claimed to be in touch with the dead have been, at other times, conscious of using their own ESP. Thus, Swedenborg "saw" a fire raging in Stockholm while he was in Gothenburg, some 300 miles away. He told an assembled group that the fire had stopped a few doors from his own house, which proved to be the case. Here Swedenborg presumably had a clairvoyant vision unrelated to departed spirits.

In the same way, psychic people have foretold the

future, or read people's minds (for example, Jeane Dixon, the so-called seeress of Washington) without invoking the aid of spirits.

However, this super-ESP hypothesis creates knotty problems of its own.

It may cover some cases of mediumistic communication—as, for example, the message Arthur Ford gave to Dr. Horlacher, ostensibly from his college friend, in which all the facts mentioned by Ford were known to the recipient and could have been picked telepathically from his mind.

Similarly, in the Swedenborg case involving the Queen of Sweden, the secret she shared with her dead brother may have been extracted from her mind by telepathy.

The telepathy hypothesis is stretched to the breaking point, however, by the communication from Upton Sinclair's wife. Remember that Sinclair himself was not present when the message came through Arthur Ford. Nor was he aware that his wife had suffered three light strokes. This was known only to the doctors who had conducted the autopsy and, therefore, if telepathy was going on, it must have been between the medium and one or more of these doctors.

But, the evidence we have on telepathy indicates that it generally flows between people who are in some way emotionally linked, or at least known to each other. Perfect strangers, it seems, rarely share a telepathic experience. There is no reason, however, to think that Arthur Ford had any emotional link with the doctors who conducted the autopsy, nor indeed that he even knew of their existence.

Conceivably, the link was provided by Upton Sinclair, who had known the medium some years before. The telepathy may have reached the doctors via Sinclair—what the French call *telepathy à trois*, or mind-reading once removed.

Telepathy cannot account for the case in which Swedenborg discovered the missing receipt, since there was no living mind which knew the information. Nor would clairvoyance, as commonly understood, seem to fit here.

Clairvoyance generally takes the form of awareness of a distant event, as though by a kind of mental television; or the reading of the contents of an opaque envelope, say. Neither of these forms of ESP would seem to apply to what happened in the missing receipt case.

However, there are other forms of clairvoyance which might apply. In what is called *psychometry*, a psychically gifted individual can pick up from a personal object facts about its present, or a previous, owner. It is as though the object has a record of past events imprinted on it and, somehow, the medium experiences a playback of these events in his mind. There is also a form of clairvoyance, not all that different, called *retrocognition*—the opposite of precognition—in which the medium perceives past events as though they were happening in the present. (It may indeed be, as some have suggested, that retrocognition is merely a species of psychometry in which the object linked with the past is an old house or a particular location instead of, say, a watch or a bracelet.)

Theoretically, psychometric or retrocognitive clairvoyance could explain Swedenborg's finding of the lost receipt. But some researchers would argue that this type of remarkably specific clairvoyance is hardly less difficult to believe than communication with the dead.

How many mediums are there who, on demand, could find, by ESP, a lost object, as Swedenborg did the missing receipt? Probably very few. If Swedenborg's feat was actually clairvoyance, it was, then, a singularly rare and efficient sort. Super-ESP, to be sure.

In the case of Olga Worrall's prediction, an alternative explanation to communication with the dead is precognition by the medium. After all, Jeane Dixon makes accurate predictions without claiming to be in touch with departed spirits.

However, the fact that Arthur Ford came up with the same prediction independently, and that in both instances the messages were in keeping with the personalities of the alleged communicators (deceased priests who had known the Reverend Robert Lewis, and been interested in his career) is compatible with the view that the two predictions were inspired by interested parties on the other side.

There are facts which seem to favor the super-ESP hypothesis and raise problems for the survival theory. One is that some spirit communicators who claimed to be dead have turned out to be embarrassingly alive.

Soon after World War II, Rosalind Heywood, a noted British psychical researcher, at an anonymous sitting with a medium mentally asked about the fate of a German friend of whom she had heard nothing since before the war. Almost immediately, as though in answer to her unspoken thoughts, the medium mentioned the friend's first name, said he was present, and that he wished to communicate.

There followed an evidential message in which were described recollections shared by the sitter. The communicator concluded by saying that he had died in rather grim circumstances about which he refused to elaborate.

All in all, the session impressed Rosalind Heywood as being quite convincing.

However, when she then made inquiries about her friend through normal channels she discovered that he was alive and well.[9]

Here, it appears that a pseudopersonality similar to that of the dead friend was molded, no doubt unconsciously, by the medium's ESP out of information filched from the sitter's mind.

There are other cases in which pseudospirits have created a dramatically realistic impression, sometimes even reproducing recognizable idiosyncrasies.

Dr. S. G. Soal, a noted mathematician and psychical researcher, once received a communication through the medium, Mrs. Blanche Cooper, which purportedly came from a school friend of his named Gordon Davis. Besides giving correct information, this communicator spoke with a dignified diction which prompted Soal to remark: "By Jove, it *is* like Gordon Davis!"

However, on checking, it was found that the friend was still living, though in Mrs. Cooper's trance the personality claiming to be Gordon Davis said he had shuffled off this mortal coil.

Spiritualists explain cases such as these as "possession by the living," the claim being that a person's astral self (or spirit) can leave his body during sleep, hypnosis, or at other times, and manifest through a medium. Another spiritualist explanation is that of "deceiving spirits" who impersonate the individuals they claim to be.

More plausible than these theories—which beg the

[9] Rosalind Heywood, "Death and Psychical Research," in *Man's Concern with Death* (London, Hodder & Stoughton, 1968).

question by assuming the thing to be proven, namely, the existence of spirits—is one which says that the medium's unconscious dramatizing powers, combined with ESP, can construct a pseudopersonality more or less resembling the communicator it claims to be.

Consider an analogy. A hypnotized subject, told that he is Napoleon, Julius Caesar, or even King Kong, can hand in a heroic performance of being that personage. How plausible the performance is depends, among other things, on how much the hypnotized subject knows about the character he is impersonating. If the subject were a medium, with powerful ESP, he might by this means discover enough obscure knowledge about the character to present a startlingly convincing impersonation.

A medium in a self-induced trance is in a highly suggestible state, and the sitter's thoughts and expectations, spoken or unspoken, can color the medium's utterances. If the sitter deliberately asks for an imaginary niece named Bessie Beals, as psychologist Stanley Hall once did with Mrs. Piper, the imaginary Miss Beals may suddenly start communicating, as indeed she did. In such a case the medium's unconscious, in collaboration with the sitter, has dramatized a figment of imagination into a "spirit."

Does this mean that all purported spirit communicators are purely subjective creations?

This conclusion does not at all follow from the evidence, any more than the existence of some fictional characters in books means that *all* characters in books are fictional. One cannot always tell, to be sure, which characters are fact and which are fiction by their mere superficial plausibility. (Hitler, after all, is a more *implausible* human monster than Bluebeard.) The only test of fiction vis à vis fact is evidence. And so it is with mediumistic communicators.

Actually, if human nature is such that it survives death, the phenomenon of partially or wholly false mediumistic communicators is what one might reasonably expect. A nonphysical entity, while still attached to a physical body, presumably would be able to range fairly far and wide, plucking facts from here and there, though not quite everywhere. The problem is to distinguish those facts which point to a genuine communicator from those which appear to be only the product of the medium's own ESP.

The problem is not unlike that of distinguishing between genuinely precognitive dreams and those which are merely Freudian. Distinguishing between them before the fact—that is to say, in the case of a precognitive dream, before its fulfillment—is very difficult, but some people do develop a fairly reliable sense of whether a dream is psychic at the time they dream it.

In somewhat the same way, experienced psychical researchers, after weighing a particular alleged communication from the dead, often are able to form a judgment as to whether it is genuine or spurious.

The survivalist theory can be reconciled with the fact of deceptively convincing pseudocommunicators by what is called the "Persona theory." Proposed formally by Dr. Hornell Hart (although anticipated by other researchers), this postulates that mediumistic trance-personalities are built up by telepathic collaboration between the unconscious dramatizing powers of the medium and those of the sitters; or—and this is crucial—between those powers of the medium and *those of a discarnate spirit*.

Basic to the Persona theory is the view that when the dead communicate they do so by telepathy and not by directly "possessing" the medium's organism. If such possession did happen, with the fullness of control it seems to imply, one would expect mediumistic communications to be uniformly lucid, coherent, and undistorted, when in fact, only rarely are they even approximately these things. More commonly, mediumistic communications are relatively slow, confused, disjointed—very much the way telepathy is. Some facts come through clearly, others are scrambled. And the communicators themselves complain that they are not in a "normal" state when they manifest through a medium; one likened it to dictating to an obtuse secretary through a door of frosted glass.

Some trance personalities claim that there is a constant danger of the medium's own unconscious thoughts and feelings muddying the communication. On the other hand, the medium's unconscious is all the communicator has to work with, the evidence suggesting that a communicator is limited, to a considerable extent, by the materials available in the medium's mind.

Thus, a woman's deceased daughter, purportedly communicating through the British medium, Ena Twigg, called her father "Wotan" when his name actually was "Wogan." (Wotan, of course, was the Viking god of war.) If the name were picked from the sitter's mind by telepathy it might more likely have been correct. However, the communicator said she *had* to use "Wotan" for that was all that was available in the medium's unconscious.

"Wasn't it clever of me, Mummy, to get his name through?" the child communicator boasted. "I couldn't find the name in the medium's mind so I thought of doing it like this. Wasn't it clever of me?" [10]

[10] Roy Stemman, *Medium Rare* (London, The Spiritualist Association of Great Britain, 1971).

To return to the Persona theory—a Persona, then, is a personality construct which can be either wholly or partly fictitious, or wholly or partly *veridical*. If it is veridical, this means that an actual surviving spirit is manifesting through a temporary facsimile of his earth personality built up by a collaboration between his discarnate mind and the unconscious mind of the medium.

It follows, from this theory, that a communicator's Persona will never be absolutely identical to his earth personality (apart altogether from the fact that people change, as much after death, presumably, as before) but always must be more or less an approximation of it.

The crucial test of the genuineness of a communicator is the impression he makes on those who knew him in life. Always allowing for possible ESP by the medium, does the communicator ring uniquely true? Is the characteristic diction there, or at least hints of it? Does he demonstrate familiarity with memories shared by the sitter? Do the little nuances which make a person as individual as a fingerprint come through, however attenuated or blurred they may become by this process of communication?

Ultimately, the only "proof" of the genuineness of a communicator is highly personal and therefore difficult —nay, impossible—to get across to another individual. How could you prove to a radical skeptic that the person you are talking to on the phone really is your wife and not some ingenious impostor? After all the obvious reasons have been cited, there remains an incommunicable residue of certainty which is yours alone.

However, though objective proof of communication with the dead may be unattainable, some psychical researchers believe that there are types of cases which virtually exclude telepathy and/or clairvoyance by the medium.

One such is the "proxy sitting" in which a person visits a medium on behalf of another individual who is not present. This stretches the telepathy hypothesis to the breaking point, and beyond, since, as I've intimated, the indications are that telepathy generally operates between two people who are linked emotionally; also, it usually means a straightforward tapping of one person's mind by another.

In proxy sittings, where the medium brings forth information for an unknown person who is not present, this would be telepathy of a peculiarly roundabout sort. And telepathy seems even less likely when the person for whom the sitter serves as proxy is not once but *twice removed*. Here is just such a case.

Dr. E. R. Dodds, at the time regius professor of Greek at Oxford University (and, incidentally, a disbeliever in survival), asked a Methodist clergyman, the Reverend Drayton Thomas, to take a proxy sitting with the medium, Mrs. Osborne Leonard. The sitting was on behalf not of Professor Dodds but a friend of his, a Mrs. Lewis, who was unknown to Thomas.

All the clergyman was told, to give to the medium, was the name, home town, and place of death of the person whom Mrs. Lewis wished to contact—her father, a Mr. Macauley, who had been a water engineer.

This minimal information was enough for Mrs. Leonard's trance control, "Feda" (said to be the spirit of a young girl), to produce a wealth of evidential personalia about Mr. Macauley.

Feda described his tools and drawing office, mentioned his concern with saving water, gave his pet name for his daughter ("Puggy"), referred to his having injured a hand, and cited the names of several persons he had known on earth who were now with him. (None of these names was common, one being Rees, described as that of a school chum of the dead man.)

Drayton Thomas, the proxy sitter, had no idea whether this information was accurate or a jumble of nonsense. However, Mrs. Lewis confirmed that all the items given by the medium were correct.[11]

In a case like this, telepathy, or clairvoyance, seems to some researchers less plausible than communication with the dead.

The problem with the super-ESP theory is the same as with the hypothetical universal solvent for which no container is conceivable. If a super-ESP faculty exists, of the scope required for mediums to ferret out facts from every obscure nook and cranny in the cosmos, then why cannot a medium simply tell anybody anything they want to know? Super-ESP is really nothing less than a pseudonym for omniscience. As a counterhypothesis to communication with the dead it has the paradoxical flaws of explaining too much, and not enough.

Another sort of case in which telepathy or clairvoyance in the medium seems an unlikely explanation involves what Dr. Ian Stevenson, head of the division of parapsychology at the University of Virginia medical school, calls "drop in" communicators. These are communicators unknown to either the medium or the sitter.

"Such communications," says Stevenson, "make even more difficult the hypothesis of telepathy from the living for explaining the results."

---

[11] Heywood, "Death and Psychical Research."

Drop-in communicators, being unknown to both medium and sitter, do not represent any emotional links, or pathways of association, along which telepathy normally seems to flow.

Stevenson describes a case of such a drop-in communicator.

The sitting took place in Zurich, Switzerland, on February 2, 1962. The medium was Frau P. Schulz, a nonprofessional who for many years had given sittings to a private circle. Present were three regular sitters: Frau N. von Muralt, and Herr and Frau Professor W. Brunner.

The communicator who dropped in identified himself as "Hans-Peter," adding that he was called that now though formerly he had had another first name. He said his surname was "Indian"—it sounded to the sitters like "Pasona."

The communicator further reported that he had died in Zurich's children's hospital from an ailment of "the appendix," describing it as "an unusual illness with a lot of fever." He had dark hair and dark eyes, he said, and two brothers still living. His father "had something to do with tea." He sent his love to his mother.

Investigation discovered a family in Zurich named Passanah, in the tea-importing business, with two sons living and one who had died of appendicitis in 1932 in the city's Kinderspital (Children's Hospital). The dead son's name was Robert.

When Ian Stevenson later made his own independent verification of the case he found that the appendicitis mentioned as the cause of the boy's death was misinformation. Robert Passanah actually had died of severe pneumonia with complications which affected the heart. This illness, said Stevenson, himself a physician, could fairly be called "unusual," as the medium said; and the boy had run a continuous high fever, so the reference to "lots of fever" was similarly accurate.

Stevenson, to his own satisfaction, ruled out the possibility that the medium had picked up the information normally. Since the boy had died some three decades before, the supposition that the medium got her data from an obituary notice seemed somewhat farfetched. Besides, that would not have provided the information that the family were tea importers.

The only remotely plausible alternative theory to communication with the dead in this case would appear to be cryptomnesia—hidden memory. In other words, the medium possibly had read the obituary notice 30 years before and the information had lain dormant in her unconscious mind until suddenly surfacing during the trance sitting. The fact that the family business was tea could have been discovered normally from other sources and similarly buried.

However, as a psychiatrist, Dr. Stevenson considers a latency period of 30 years barely plausible. In most cases of cryptomnesia, he says, the buried memory surfaces relatively soon after registering in the unconscious.

A careful shifting of the evidence led Ian Stevenson to "favor the idea that a real discarnate communicator influenced this communication." [12]

And a careful sifting of all the evidence presented in this chapter leads, I believe, to the conclusion that human beings on the other side of death have established through mediumistic communication that they still live; and that

[12] Ian Stevenson, "A Communicator Unknown to Mediums and Sitters," *Journal of the American Society for Psychical Research,* Vol. 64 (January, 1970).

self-consciousness, memory, love, purpose, and other attributes of personality are at least as strong in the next world as they are here.

Now on to further evidence.

CHAPTER 3

The Evidence from Apparitions

An English couple were getting ready to retire for the night when the woman looked up and was astonished to see an unfamiliar man in a peaked cap leaning on the bedpost staring intently at her.

"Willie," the woman said in a hoarse whisper, and her husband, who had been looking the other way, turned toward the intruder. His face paled and he demanded: "What on earth are you doing here?"

With that, the figure drew himself into an upright position and said, in a commanding, peculiarly hollow voice: "Willie, Willie!" The tone was reproachful, even exasperated.

Then the figure turned and walked slowly toward the wall. As it passed in front of a lamp the couple noticed that it blocked off the light. The figure melted into the wall.

The husband, in great agitation, searched the house but found no sign of an intruder.

Later, he told his wife that the figure was his deceased father, whom she had never known. He said that in young manhood his father had been a naval officer, a fact he had never mentioned before. He also admitted to his wife that he was involved in a shaky business deal and felt that his father was expressing disapproval.[1]

[1] G. N. M. Tyrell, *Apparitions* (New York, Collier Books, 1963).

This incident, reported by the distinguished British psychical researcher, G. N. M. Tyrrell, is a classic instance of what is called an apparition. It is classic because the apparitional figure had most, if not all, of the characteristics which recur in the best cases.

To start with, the apparition was perfectly lifelike, resembling so closely a flesh-and-blood person as to be virtually indistinguishable from one. It cast a shadow and blocked off light, as when it passed in front of the lamp. And yet, though appearing solid enough to touch, it melted through the wall. In this instance, the apparition was perceived by more than one person.

On the night of June 11, 1923, in Indianapolis, Mrs. Gladys Watson, the daughter of a Methodist clergyman, was awakened from a deep sleep by someone quietly but insistently calling her name. As she roused and sat up, she was astonished to see her paternal grandfather, to whom she was devoted, leaning toward her. He looked perfectly real and lifelike. There was a pleasant smile on his face.

"Don't be frightened," he reassured her in a warm, affectionate voice. "It's only me. I've just died."

Mrs. Watson found tears starting in her eyes and she instinctively reached across the bed to rouse her sleeping husband.

"This is how they'll bury me," her grandfather said, indicating the dark suit and black bow tie he was wearing. He added: "I just wanted to tell you I've been waiting to go ever since mother was taken."

The Watson house was next door to the Lilly Laboratories and the bedroom was dimly illuminated by light from the laboratory windows. Gladys Watson could see that her grandfather looked as solid as though he were physically present in the room. And she heard his voice not with an inner ear but as though he were actually speaking to her.

She reached across and shook her husband again. This time he woke up, rubbed his eyes and sat up in bed. The apparition had vanished.

Mr. Watson declared that his wife had had a vivid nightmare.

"Your grandfather is alive and well with your folks in Wilmington," he insisted.

But his wife refused to accept that her experience had been a dream. Finally, to prove his point, Watson got out of bed and phoned his wife's parents in Wilmington.

The call was answered by Gladys Watson's mother. The phone had not awakened her, she said, because she already was awake and in fact had been about to call the Watsons to tell them the sad news that Grandfather Parker had died a short time before, at four o'clock.

Mrs. Watson, when the apparition awakened her, had glanced at the clock beside the bed. It said four o'clock.[2]

This apparition significantly differed from the previous one only in the fact that it was perceived by a single person (whether the percipient's husband also would have seen it if he had awakened in time is a moot point). As in the previous case, however, the figure appeared life-like, not misty or ethereal. (It is significant, in this respect, that the light from the nearby Lilly Laboratories was observed to illumine the apparition as well as the other objects in the room; in other words, it was not self-illuminated, any more than an actual person would have been.)

[2] Laura A. Dale, "A Series of Spontaneous Cases in the Tradition of Phantasms of the Living," *Journal of the American Society for Psychical Research*, Vol. XLV, No. 3.

Technically, an apparition is a hallucination (a sense perception without the corresponding object) of a special sort called *veridical*, as distinguished from the ordinary sort which can be the product of drugs, delirium, hypnosis, waking dream states, or insanity.

The distinctive feature of a veridical, in contrast to a nonveridical, hallucination is that it conveys information which was not normally known. In this case, for example, the apparition of Mrs. Watson's grandfather correctly told her that he had just died, something she had no way of knowing. In the previous case, the apparition was perceived in a naval uniform by the man's wife, though she claimed not to have been aware of her deceased father-in-law's career at sea.

In both these cases, then, the apparition communicated information—in one instance verbally, in the other indirectly, by its appearance—which was not known to the percipient.

An apparition, in the sense in which the term is used by some psychical researchers, is exclusively a phenomenon of wakefulness; people see it when they are fully conscious. There are, however, appearances of the dead which, while exhibiting many of the characteristics of a classic apparition, occur not in the waking state but in dreams. These two kinds of appearances—those in wakefulness and those in dreams—should, to my mind, be considered different forms of basically the same experience. In a dream apparition, as in a waking one, the distinguishing feature is the paranormal information conveyed.

Here is a typical case of a "truth-telling" dream apparition from the files of an eminent parapsychologist, Dr. Louisa Rhine.

The experiencer was the son of a prominent attorney who had died on September 11, 1929. About a month later, a court case developed in which a central issue was a $500 loan the attorney had made to a woman. What was needed to settle the case was the written agreement in which the woman had promised to repay the loan in monthly installments. This was missing and the attorney's son could not find it.

One night, in a vivid dream, his father appeared to him looking young and vital.

"How are you?" he said, "I thought I'd come and pay you a visit."

"But, Dad," the son replied in his dream, "how did you get out of that concrete vault they put you in?"

"You're not talking to me," replied the father. "It's my spirit."

Then the son asked him about the missing agreement.

"I can tell you exactly where it is," the father said. "I was afraid she (the woman to whom the loan was given) would steal it. In the right-hand top drawer of my desk; you'll find it full of envelopes turned up edgeways and a piece of newspaper folded under them. Raise the newspaper and you'll find the contract in a large manila envelope. It's got my name and her name on the underside of it."

As he said this, the dream figure looked up and remarked: "It's beginning to get daylight. I've got to go."

At this point the dreamer was wakened by his wife shaking him. "You've been mumbling incoherently for I don't know how long," she whispered.

The man immediately went to his dead father's office and, following the instructions given in the dream, found the agreement which hitherto had eluded him.[8]

[8] Louisa E. Rhine, *ESP in Life and Lab* (New York, Collier Books, 1967).

This case is not unique. In the annals of psychical research the classic instance of a truth-telling dream apparition is the Chaffin Will Case, in which a "ghost" changed a court decision.

On September 7, 1921, James Chaffin, Sr., a prosperous and, by all accounts, rather eccentric farmer of Davie County, North Carolina, died as the result of a fall. His will, dated November 16, 1905, bequeathed all his worldly goods to his favorite son, Marshall, the youngest of four. His widow, and the three other sons, were left out in the cold.

Some four years later, during the month of June 1925, the dead man's second son, James, had a vivid recurring dream in which his father appeared to him. There was a look of pain, or perhaps yearning, on the dead man's face, but he never spoke—until one night when the dream came even more vividly than before.

"My father appeared at my bedside again," James Chaffin testified. "He was dressed as I had often seen him dressed in life, wearing a black overcoat which I knew to be his own. This time he spoke to me.

"He took hold of his overcoat and pulled it back and said, 'You will find my will in my overcoat pocket,' and then disappeared."

James Chaffin said he awoke feeling certain that his father's spirit had visited him to rectify a mistake which was causing him sorrow.

Chaffin went to his mother's in search of the old black overcoat his father once wore and discovered that she had given it to his brother, John, who lived in Yadkin County, some 20 miles away.

On July 6 James Chaffin, at his brother's, examined the old overcoat. The inside pocket was stitched shut. Opening it, he found a little roll of paper, tied with string, on which, in what appeared to be the dead man's handwriting, were scrawled the words: "Read the 27th chapter of Genesis in my daddie's old Bible." (The dead man's father had been a minister and his Bible was a family heirloom.)

At this point, James Chaffin, certain that he was on the verge of an important discovery, enlisted a neighbor, Thomas Blackwelder, to accompany him as a witness. Chaffin's daughter and Blackwelder's daughter also went along.

They found the Bible in the top drawer of a dresser in the widowed Mrs. Chaffin's house. As Blackwelder lifted the worn volume, it crumbled in his hands. Leafing through the portion containing the Book of Genesis he found, tucked between the pages at the designated spot, the twenty-seventh chapter—which, significantly, describes how Jacob cheated his older brother Esau out of his birthright—a document apparently in the deceased's handwriting.

It proved to be a will, dated January 16, 1919, some 14 years later than the original, and read as follows:

> After reading the 27th chapter of Genesis, I, James L. Chaffin, do make my last will and testament, and here it is. I want, after giving my body a decent burial, my little property to be equally divided between my four children, if they are living at my death, both personal and real estate divided equal, if not living, give share to their children. And if she is living, you all must take care of your mammy. Now this is my last will and testament. Witness my hand and seal. James L. Chaffin.
>
> This January 16, 1919.[4]

[4] "James Chaffin's Will," *Journal of the American Society for Psychical Research* (November, 1927).

Though unwitnessed, this will was fully valid under North Carolina law, if there was no doubt that it had been written by the testator. It was submitted to the court for probate.

Marshall Chaffin, named sole beneficiary in the previous will, had since died but his widow, acting as guardian for her son, Marshall's legal heir, contested the new will.

The case went to court in December 1925. Ten witnesses, including a professional handwriting expert, were prepared to testify that the second will was in the testator's own hand. However, no testimony was heard after Marshall Chaffin's widow, on being shown the new will, immediately acknowledged that the handwriting was indeed that of her deceased father-in-law. Accordingly, the second will was probated by the court.

Here, then, is a case in which the apparition of a dead man communicated information responsible for a legal judgment setting aside a duly probated will and enforcing another in its place.

What about possible explanations other than communication with the dead?

One theory is that the second will was a fake planted by James Chaffin, possibly with the connivance of his mother and his brothers. They did, after all, have a motive.

Admittedly, too, there are details of the story hard to understand. If James Chaffin, Sr. had been concerned enough about the injustice of his first will to write another it is curious indeed that he did not mention the second will or leave some clear directions as to where it could be found after his death.

However, he died suddenly, remember, from a fall, and

it is possible that his untimely demise prevented him from revealing the new will on his deathbed, as he may have intended to do. The older Chaffin, as already intimated, apparently had more than his share of eccentricities (for example, though affluent, he wore the same tattered black overcoat, in which the note about the second will later was found, for many years, long after most people would have given it to the Salvation Army). His odd personality presumably accounts for his not mentioning the second will. Who, really, can explain human motivations?

At any rate, the fact that 10 witnesses were prepared to swear that the handwriting in the will undoubtedly was the dead man's—and moreover, Marshall Chaffin's widow conceded it—seems to rule out any question of a hoax.

Another theory is cryptomnesia. This speculates that the Chaffin family had heard about the second will but forgot, and the buried memory later manifested in the form of the dream.

Most researchers find this idea farfetched. Is it conceivable that people who were to benefit from a will would forget about it? This is doubly unlikely when the period between the date the will was written and the testator's death was about two years, a short span for any memory. Cryptomnesia in this case is utterly improbable.

Another theory, one which accepts some sort of supernormal element, is that James Chaffin telepathically picked the information about the second will from his father's mind while the old man was still alive, but this knowledge remained latent in his unconscious until it surfaced in the form of a dream.

Such delayed or deferred telepathy is theoretically possible, I suppose, but in this instance the latency period seems to have been unduly long. Why would it take four years—the time which elapsed between the old man's death and the apparitional dreams—for the knowledge to surface into his son's conscious mind? From the published findings on telepathy it would seem that such a long latency period is virtually unheard of; and if so, what basis is there for assuming that in this particular instance telepathy acted in a manner totally different from what is known to be usual?

The most plausible interpretation of the Chaffin Will Case, I submit, is that the dead man did communicate to correct an injustice caused by his spite or carelessness.

There is another sort of apparitional experience which, for want of a better label, I will call the nonvisual type. A nonvisual apparition, I know, seems a contradiction in terms—like hearing a color, or touching a sound—but there are some analogues. For example, if a subject in deep hypnosis is told that when he awakens a certain person who was in the room will no longer be present, a curious thing occurs. The subject awakens, with no memory of the suggestion, and acts as though that person were indeed absent though, in fact, he is standing in the middle of the room. In this sort of negative hallucination, the subject cannot see that which everybody else sees. Yet, at the same time, he reports feeling strange, of having an "uncanny" (this is the word one subject used) sense of a presence in the room.

This sense of "presence" is very real to the person experiencing it. In the case of the subject who is acting out a posthypnotic suggestion it arises presumably from the fact that though his eyes actually see the person who is supposed to be invisible, his mind, obeying the suggestion given, refuses to translate that retinal image into visual perception. However, he has the subliminal sense of something seen yet not seen, lurking just beyond vision.

There are experiences in which perfectly sane, normal people have had a similar "uncanny" sense of the presence of a dead loved one or friend. They do not see the person, though feeling that at any moment they might. But someone, they sense, *is there* and *ought* to be visible.

Here is such a case reported by an unusually impressive witness, Dr. C. G. Jung, the celebrated psychiatrist. Jung was singularly competent, surely, to distinguish probable fact from fantasy in such experiences. In this instance, he had a nonvisual vision, as it were, of a dead friend.

"One night," Jung says, "I lay awake thinking of the sudden death of a friend whose funeral had taken place the day before. I was deeply concerned. Suddenly I felt that he was in the room. It seemed that he stood at the foot of my bed and was asking me to go with him. I did not have the feeling of an apparition; rather, it was an inner visual image of him. . . ."

Jung goes on to tell how he tried to dismiss the feeling as fantasy, but was forced to ask himself: "Do I have any proof that this is a fantasy? Suppose it is not a fantasy, suppose my friend is really here and I decided he was only a fantasy—would that not be abominable of me?"

Deciding, as an experiment, to give his deceased friend the benefit of the doubt, to credit him with reality, Jung immediately felt that he went to the door and beckoned him to follow. In his imagination, Jung went along.

The friend led him outside, through the garden to the

road, and finally to his house, which was nearby. Jung followed him into his study, where the friend climbed on a stool and indicated the second of five books with red bindings standing on the second shelf from the top. Then the vision ended.

Jung brooded on the meaning of the strange experience. He was not familiar with his dead friend's study and certainly had no idea of the titles of specific books on its shelves.

The next morning he went to the friend's widow and asked whether he might look up something in his library. There, as in the vision of the night before, was a stool standing before the bookcase, and, sure enough, on the second shelf from the top, the five books with red bindings.

Taking down the second one of the five, Jung discovered that it belonged to a series of Zola's novels in translation. Its title: *The Legacy of the Dead.*[5]

If Jung's dead friend actually did communicate, wanting to convey a sign of his continued existence, could any title have been more appropriate?

Some apparitional experiences are very dramatic, making the difference, even, between life and death. Such a case comes from Louisa Rhine's files.

The protagonists are identified only as Norman and Pete, two American soldiers, close friends, who were stationed together on Guam in 1944. Pete was killed in action against the Japanese, and three weeks later an extraordinary thing occurred.

Norman was assigned to drive several staff officers on an observation tour behind the front lines. A Marine told

[5] C. G. Jung, *Memories, Dreams, Reflections* (New York, New York Books, 1963).

him of a short cut to take on the way back to the base. About dusk, on the return trip, he came to the suggested turning-off place. He had gone only a couple of car lengths down the bumpy road when suddenly he saw Pete ahead, waving frantically for him to go back.

Norman backed his vehicle out of the side road and took the normal route back to the base. The officers in the car made no comment on his erratic driving.

It was only after he was back on the other road that Norman realized, with the sudden impact of a body blow: "That was Pete, but he's dead!" He shook his head wonderingly, and kept going.

Later he heard that a truckload of Marines who took that side road a few minutes after he turned back had been blown up by a Japanese land mine.[6]

These apparitional experiences make a strong case for intervention by the dead. Consider some of the significant features they share.

One: All the cases cited appear to show evidence of intention. There are clear signs of a motivation behind the apparitional experience—whether to warn an erring son, to inform a loved one of a death, to communicate the whereabouts of a missing document, to prove continued existence after death, or to save a friend's life.

Second: All the cases conveyed information not known to the percipient (or, in the collective case, *one* of the percipients, the naval officer's daughter-in-law).

Three: In most, though not all, of the cases, the information conveyed apparently was known to no living person, or, if it was, not to one with whom the percipient

---

[6] Louisa E. Rhine, *Hidden Channels of The Mind* (New York, William Sloane Associates, 1961).

would be likely to have had a telepathic link. (In the Norman and Pete case, for example, the Japanese troops who planted the mine certainly knew it was there but it seems unlikely that Norman unwittingly tuned in to their thoughts.)

How common are apparitions of the dead? Surprisingly common, it seems. A research psychologist in the United States and a physician in Britain, both of whom made special studies of the subject, estimate that almost 50 percent of normal people have had such an experience.

Dr. Robert Kastenbaum, on the staff of the Wayne State University Center for Psychological Studies of Dying, Death, and Lethal Behavior, said: "People who have these experiences are not mystics or spiritualists but secretaries, mailmen, barbers, factory workers, engineers, and other practical-minded persons."

Most, he said, are reluctant to discuss the experiences with anybody for fear of being thought odd, or even insane.

"There was a woman, for example," remarked Dr. Kastenbaum, "whose son-in-law had died of an overdose of heroin. One night when she went to bed she noticed that her dog refused to sleep at her feet for the first time in 11 years.

"Instead, he stood at the door of her room, growling. In the middle of the night she woke and saw her dead son-in-law sitting by her, crying.

"This woman is not easily deluded nor one taken with fancies. She knows what she saw but she could never tell anyone about it until she told us.

"We probably have a vast number of spiritual communicators among us but are not aware of them. There are more people who keep it to themselves than are willing to talk about it."

The Detroit behavioral scientist, who made a report on his studies of appearances of the dead at the annual convention of the American Psychological Association in September 1971, said that out of 140 people questioned—none of whom had any association with spiritualism or the occult—63 described "an experience which seemed, at the time, as though it involved communication with another mind, since deceased and invisible."

Similar conclusions were reached by Dr. W. Dewi Rees, a Welsh physician, who reported in the *British Medical Journal* that of 293 widows and widowers he studied, 137, or some 47 percent, admitted having experienced what seemed to be communication with their deceased spouse. One in six claimed to have seen his or her partner's "ghost."

Said Dr. Rees: "I am convinced from my study, probably the most rigorous and definitive there has been on the subject, that almost half of all widows and widowers receive messages from, and experience the presence of, their former mates even years after their death."

Apparitional experiences make a strong prima facie case for communication by the dead. Before reaching a firm conclusion, however, we should look at two types of apparitions which are different from these we have examined. One is the traditional ghost—a form of apparition which does not betray any conscious motivation; the other is an apparition of the *living*.

The classic ghost is an apparition of a special sort. First, it is usually linked to a certain place, such as an ancestral dwelling; and second, it appears to lack consciousness.

Newport

Alive with pleasure!

Newport 20 CLASS A CIGARETTES

Newport

MENTHOL KINGS

©Lorillard 1975

If you have
a taste for quality,
you'll like the taste
of Kent.

King Size
or Deluxe 100's.

KENT

WITH
THE FAMOUS MICRONITE FILTER

KING SIZE

KING SIZE
KENT

Ghosts generally perform the same ritualistic acts over and over—like a rerun on television. In the view of many parapsychologists, ghosts, as a rule, are not in any sense conscious but rather are images from the past. This concept, called the psychometric theory of hauntings, likens the ghost who lurks in the same old castle century after century to the psychic impressions which cling to a personal object, such as a watch or pen, and can be sensed by a psychometrist. Every object associated with people has memories—especially, it seems, old houses.

Dr. Nandor Fodor, the psychoanalyst-ghost hunter, said:

> It seems as if emotion, if it has been very deep—anguish, particularly—leaves an impression in the house where it was endured. And . . . it is possible that somehow an attuning takes place and as if on a screen, by a kind of etheric television, suddenly a scene from the past becomes visible.
>
> I say from the past because usually the so-called ghost walks on floor levels which no longer exist or on non-existent staircases. So quite visibly it does not come from our present age but is a kind of projection from the past.[7]

If a ghost, then, represents the playback of emotion-charged events recorded in some psychic ether, it possesses no more consciousness than the images on a motion picture film. In this respect it differs radically from apparitions which do appear to represent intention, as in the case of the dead father communicating the whereabouts of his will.

(A few ghostly apparitions seem to have exhibited in-

[7] Allen Spraggett, *The Unexplained* (New York, New American Library, 1967).

tention and self-consciousness, but on the whole, placed-oriented spooks best fit the psychometric theory.)

Apparitions of living people form another category to consider. Most common here are so-called crisis apparitions which appear to be triggered by some emotion-laden event or stressful situation. The great British psychical researcher, F. W. H. Myers, reported many such cases.

A woman identified by Myers as the Honorable Miss K. Ward recalled waking up one morning about eight o'clock to see her sister, Emily, whose room was just across the hall, sitting at the foot of her bed. Emily was in a nightgown and rocking back and forth as though in great pain. As Miss Ward put out her hand to touch her, the figure vanished.

Later Miss Ward discovered that at eight o'clock her sister had been in severe pain—though the night before she had felt perfectly well—and was seated on the bed in her nightgown rocking back and forth, just as she appeared in the vision.[8]

There are numerous cases in which the likeness of a living individual has appeared, as in this instance, to another person. Usually the appearer had no idea the apparition occurred. As intimated, this sort of unconscious projection of an apparition appears to be provoked by strong emotion. Or it may occur while the appearer is in a state of altered consciousness, whether a trance, drug stupor, coma, or even sleep.

Here is a recent case, which I personally documented, of an unconscious apparition. The people involved want anonymity, but the facts are exactly as set down.

The incident occurred on August 1, 1972, between 3:30

[8] F. W. H. Myers, *Human Personality and Its Survival of Bodily Death* (London, Longmans Green & Co., 1903).

and 4 P.M., in a suburb of Toronto. Two housewives were chatting on the back patio of one of their homes. The day was warm and bright.

Suddenly one of the women said: "There's Dick"—Dick being her husband. The neighbor, too, saw him. He was in his own backyard next door.

Dick, a clergyman, was in a pair of white shorts which he often wore in the summer, and no shirt. The neighbor remarked on his good tan and, idly, asked his wife why she didn't buy him a pair of colored shorts for a change.

Dick was visible to both women for about five minutes. Then they saw him turn and walk back toward his house, disappearing behind a hillside.

When Dick's wife entered their house about 20 minutes later she was surprised to find him stretched out on the bed asleep as he had been when she left him. He still had on a blue sports shirt and blue trousers that he had worn the previous night during an all-night drive from Philadelphia to Toronto. He seemed to be in an exhausted, almost drugged sleep.

When his wife awakened him, Dick insisted that he had not been out in the yard a few minutes before. And as for wearing his white shorts—where *were* they? He said he didn't know.

Dick owned only two pairs of white shorts. The women agreed that the pair he was wearing when they saw him had an elasticized back. That particular pair turned out to be at the bottom of the laundry basket, jammed in under dirty sheets and blankets. Dick's wife said she remembered putting them there more than a week earlier. The second pair of white shorts was still packed in Dick's suitcase; he had taken them on vacation but had not worn them. They were smooth and uncreased.

What happened here?

The first possibility that will occur to any ordinarily skeptical person is that the whole incident was a practical joke. However, Dick and his wife and their neighbor insist that it was not a joke.

The second possibility is mistaken identity. But the only man in the neighborhood who even remotely resembled Dick was out of town for the day. Besides, the two women insisted they could not possibly have been mistaken in their identification.

Another possibility is that Dick walked in his sleep, undressed, donned his white shorts (after first digging them out of the laundry basket), went outside, came back in, doffed the shorts, redressed himself, and got back into bed—all without awakening or being aware of what he was doing.

Arguing against this theory is the fact that Dick, so far as he or his wife knows, has never walked or even talked in his sleep. And a psychoanalyst told me that the odds were strongly against a person with no history of somnambulism suddenly becoming a full-blown sleepwalker. Dick also is a refractory hypnotic subject, and has never experienced unaccountable lapses of memory, both of which indicate that he is not unusually suggestible nor prone to dissociation or automatism. (Dissociation and automatism pertain to acts carried out while the individual is in a distracted state of consciousness and of which he has no recollection later.)

A fourth possibility—and one which brings us to the question of what, precisely, an apparition is—rests on the assumption that the incident was a shared hallucination. In other words, Dick's wife and the neighbor (who is married to a doctor) projected the figure out of their minds, in the same way that a hypnotized person can be made to see a pink elephant or anything else.

The only weakness with this theory, said the psycho-analyst I consulted, is that collective hallucinations are "exceedingly rare," though apparently they do happen.

If this *were* a case of a double hallucination, what triggered it? Why should both women suddenly see, and watch for a full five minutes, the same hallucinated figure?

One possible answer is that the origin of the hallucination was a telepathic impulse transmitted from the mind of Dick, while he was sleeping, to his wife. She, in turn, unconsciously, by a kind of psychic contagion, telepathically transmitted the hallucination to the neighbor sitting beside her, so that both saw virtually the same thing.

What evidence is there that telepathy *can* project hallucinations?

Well, there are cases of experimental apparitions in which people have successfully willed a likeness of themselves—or, rarely, of somebody else—to appear to a distant person. Consider two cases reported by F. W. H. Myers.

A woman whom Myers knew, named Edith Danvers, claimed to have had some success in projecting a personal likeness over a considerable distance. Myers asked her to make herself appear to a friend, Mrs. Fleetwood, without forewarning that person, and to send him a letter telling him of the attempt before knowing whether it had been successful or not.

On June 20, 1894, Myers received a card from Edith Danvers, dated three days before, saying that at twelve o'clock that night she had tried to appear to Mrs. Fleetwood who lived some nine miles away.

"I succeeded in feeling that I was really in her room," Miss Danvers reported.

Myers also received a memorandum from Mrs. Fleetwood declaring that on June 17, at midnight, she awoke to see Edith Danvers "apparently kneeling on an easy chair by my bedside . . . her hair flowing, her eyes closed."

In actual fact, Edith Danvers, while she was attempting the projection, did have her hair down and her eyes closed, as Mrs. Fleetwood said, though she was reclining rather than kneeling.

There seems to have been more than a coincidental connection between Edith Danvers's attempt to project herself and her friend's vision. The odds against a person just happening to have such a hallucination at the very time another was trying to transmit one are astronomical.

In another case Myers describes how a man named H. M. Wesermann had made numerous attempts to transmit mental images to sleeping friends—that is to say, to impress dreams upon them—and had been successful on four occasions. (That such a thing can be done, and no doubt *is* being done unawares every night by some of us, is demonstrated by research at the Menninger Dream Laboratory of Brooklyn's Maimonides Medical Center, where in four experiments out of every seven, subjects have succeeded in telepathically influencing the dreams of other subjects.[9])

Wesermann's next attempt resulted in an apparition, not of himself—for, wanting to try something different, this was not his aim—but of a woman who had been dead for five years. The intention in Wesermann's mind was that in a dream this woman should appear to a lieutenant whom Wesermann knew.

In a written account of what happened that night, the lieutenant reported that he and a friend staying overnight

[9] M. Ullman and S. Krippner, *Dream Studies and Telepathy: An Experimental Approach*, Parapsychological Monographs No. 12 (Parapsychology Foundation, 1970).

in his apartment suddenly saw the door open and a woman, whom neither had ever seen before, enter the room.

"She was," the lieutenant said, "very pale, about five feet four inches in height, strong and broad of figure, dressed in white, but with a large black kerchief which reached to below the waist."

The woman nodded to the two men, then turned and left the room. A hasty search revealed no trace of the woman nor of any hoax.

The description given by the lieutenant matched the appearance of the dead woman whose image Wesermann was trying to project.

Let us summarize the facts about apparitions and relate them directly to the question of communication with the dead.

We have seen, in the cases considered, that apparitions, or appearances of the dead, whether during wakefulness or sleep, can communicate meaningful information unknown to the recipient (and which, in some cases, apparently could *never* have been discovered normally).

We also have seen that apparitions of the living as well as of the dead, occur, and in some cases these can be deliberately produced by a person with the necessary gift or acquired skill.

These facts lead to two major conclusions.

First, the most plausible explanation for most (though not all) apparitions is that they are hallucinations induced in the percipient by a telepathic impulse. This impulse may be either unconscious or deliberate on the part of the sender.

Second, if apparitions of the living come from the minds of living people, whence come apparitions of the dead? The most likely conclusion is that they are projections from the minds of dead people.

When, for example, James Chaffin, Jr., saw his father in a dream and received from him the information which led to discovery of the second will, it is reasonable—from what we know about telepathic apparitions of the living—to surmise that this appearance originated with the dead man who projected the image of himself from his discarnate mind into his son's incarnate mind.

This agrees with the hypothesis about mediumistic communications favored in the previous chapter, namely, that the dead communicate not by "possessing" the medium's organism but by telepathically projecting thoughts into his mind. The evidence, in the case of apparitions of the dead, that these are telepathic images rather than actual spirit entities lies in the fact that the information communicated usually shows the same kind of distortion as commonly occurs in mediumistic messages.

When, for example, James Chaffin, Jr., heard his father speak to him, the apparition saying, "You will find my will in my overcoat pocket," the statement was not precisely accurate. What was in the overcoat pocket proved to be not the will but the note which led to the will. This may seem a minor point but it is significant for, surely, if what James Chaffin saw and heard was his dead father's actual spirit, one would expect the communication to have been absolutely correct. However, if it were a telepathic impression projected from his deceased father's mind into his own, with all the attendant distortions to which we know telepathy is subject, this slight error in the information makes sense.

The evidence, then, points to the conclusion that apparitions of the dead are, in most cases, telepathic projections from discarnate minds to incarnate minds for the purpose of communicating either specific information or a general statement, such as that life does go on after death.

To be sure, there are some quasi-apparitions, or apparition-like experiences, which do not fit any of the categories we have examined in this chapter. These are out-of-the-body, or psychic projection, experiences which offer additional cogent evidence of man's survival of death.

Let's now look at this evidence.

CHAPTER 4

The Evidence from
Out-of-the-Body Experiences
and Temporary Death

George Ritchie, Jr., medically died on December 20, 1943. And every time he tells about the experience, in a sense he re-dies that death.

This psychiatrist from Charlottesville, Virginia, was in a state of clinical death for almost 10 minutes. During that period he was not unconscious, as appearances certainly indicated, but actually more conscious, more aware, he says, than he had ever been.

Ritchie reports that during his pseudodeath experience he glimpsed another world, another dimension of existence, in a series of blinding panoramic images which culminated in a luminous vision of a Presence.

This experience, he says, permanently erased any fear of death, for death, he now believes, is merely another face of life.

George Ritchie, who holds a medical degree from the Medical College of Virginia and took his psychiatric specialization at the University of Virginia, told me about his temporary death on a television program of which I was host. He also showed me—and I have photostatic copies of them—two notarized statements, one signed by

Donald G. Francy, M.D., of Lyndhurst, New Jersey, the other by a nurse, Retta Irvine of Nueces County, Texas, attesting to Ritchie's journey into death and back.

In his affidavit, Dr. Francy describes what he calls the "supra-mundane" experience of Private George Ritchie of the United States Army.

"I was a medical officer stationed at Camp Barkley, Texas, and was in charge of three of the isolation wards at the Camp Barkley Station Hospital in December of 1943," Dr. Francy states.

He goes on to tell how Private Ritchie, then 19 years old, was admitted to the base hospital on December 11, 1943, suffering from "acute naso-pharyngitis" (nose and throat infection). The patient at first appeared to respond to antibiotic therapy but then his condition worsened and was diagnosed as "severe lobar pneumonia."

In the early hours of December 20, the patient, according to Dr. Francy's statement, "was extremely toxic and delirious." The enlisted man who served as ward attendant thought Ritchie had stopped breathing.

"The medical officer examined the patient," Dr. Francy's affidavit continues, "and could detect no evidence of respiration or cardiac impulse and stated that the patient had expired and gave orders to the ward attendant to prepare the body for transmission to the morgue."

However, after a period of some nine minutes, the ward attendant thought he detected slight chest movements in the dead man and again summoned the medical officer.

"He administered adrenalin into the heart," reports Dr. Francy, "and Private Ritchie began to evidence increase in respiration and developed perceptible pulse."

On January 8, 1944, the "dead" man was discharged from the hospital.

Dr. Francy concludes his statement with this judgment:

> These are the facts concerning Private George C. Ritchie's critical illness as I recall them and, speaking for myself, I feel sure that his virtual call from death and return to vigorous health has to be explained in terms other than natural means (or causes).

The physician's account is supported by the statement of Retta Irvine, the nurse who attended George Ritchie during his return trip into death.

She says:

> I remember that this patient was pronounced dead at two different times by the medical officer who was on duty, yet after he was given an injection into the heart muscle the patient revived and in due time regained his health. During his convalescence Pvt. Ritchie asked me how near dead he had been. When I told him what had happened he said he thought that he had been dead. Although he did not go into detail he told me that he had had an experience that would probably change his life.

The experience which changed George Ritchie's life provides shattering, first-person evidence that human beings never really die.

At the height of his medical crisis, Ritchie recalls, he suddenly felt no longer sick but exhilarated. He sprang out of bed. Then he noticed something which jarred him.

"Someone was lying on the bed I had just left," he said. "I stepped closer in the dim light, then drew back. He was dead. The slack jaw, the gray skin were awful. Then I saw the ring. On his left hand was the Phi Gamma Delta fraternity ring I had worn for two years."

There followed a period of acute confusion in which Ritchie, incredulous, tried to assimilate the fact that there were two of him—one, obviously dead, lying on the bed, the other observing. Realization slowly dawned.

"This is death," he thought. "This is what we human beings call death, this splitting up of one's self. It was the first time I had connected death with what had happened to me."

Then George Ritchie sensed a presence beside him.

"The little room began to fill with light. I say 'light' but there is no word in our language to describe brilliance that intense. . . . That room was flooded, pierced, illuminated by the most total compassion I had ever felt. It was a presence so comforting, so joyous and all-satisfying, that I wanted to lose myself forever in the wonder of it."

In a split second, he seemed to see all the episodes of his life unreeling before him and he was stabbed by the urgent question: "What did you do with your time on earth?"

The walls of the hospital room then seemed to dissolve, to drop away, and George Ritchie said he had a sense of being transported into other dimensions.

"I saw a city—but a city, if such a thing is conceivable, constructed out of light. At that time I had not read the Book of Revelation in the Bible, nor, incidentally, anything on the subject of life after death.

"But here was a city in which the walls, houses, streets, seemed to give off light, while moving among them were beings of pure light.

"This was only a moment's vision for the next instant the walls of the hospital room closed around me, the dazzling light faded, and a strange sleep stole over me. . . ."

As he told me about his unusual experience George Ritchie, shrugging, confessed: "To this day I cannot fully fathom why I was chosen to return to life. All I know is that when I woke up in that hospital bed it was not a homecoming. . . ."

A pathologist from a large hospital, who was on the television show with Dr. Ritchie, commented that, although such current definitive measures of death as "a flat EEG" would be more conclusive, a patient showing the signs Ritchie did could only be considered dead. The pathologist added that in his years of experience with death he had never encountered, nor heard of, a case so unusual as George Ritchie's.

In actual fact, however, Ritchie's experience was not unique, nor even all that rare. It is typical of a whole class of phenomena known as out-of-the-body experiences, or, among psychical researchers, OBE for short. This case differs from the norm only in that it is better documented than most because of the particular circumstances.

Not all out-of-the-body experiences involve pseudo-death, though many do. The case of Leslie Sharpe, which opens this book, is a recent example of what his doctors suggested was "the experience of the soul leaving the body."

Some notables have experienced out-of-the-bodiness.

Author Ernest Hemingway, as a youth of 19, was serving in the armed forces in Italy during World War I when, about midnight, on July 8, 1918, he was in a trench near the village of Fossalta and an Austrian mortar shell landed nearby.

"I felt my soul or something coming right out of my body," Hemingway told his friend Guy Hickok, European correspondent for the Brooklyn *Daily Eagle*, "like you'd pull a silk handkerchief out of a pocket by one corner. It flew around and then came back in and I wasn't dead any more."

As it was, Hemingway received serious wounds. Later he used this personal experience in his novel, *A Farewell to Arms*, when his hero, Frederick Henry, is in a trench and suddenly there is an explosion nearby and Henry describes how "I felt myself rush bodily out of myself and out and out and out and all the time bodily . . . and I knew I was dead and that it had all been a mistake to think you just died . . . I felt myself slide back . . . and I was back."

Somerset Maugham, the British novelist, described how, at the age of 80, he died in a hospital and came back. Maugham was an avowed agnostic and disbeliever in survival, but his account is all the more convincing for that.

> I began to sink [Maugham said]. . . . Time ended. It might have been an hour or a century. The light began to change. To my surprise it did not grow darker—but lighter. It became iridescent, blinding. I could sense my pulse . . . fading and my heartbeat slowing and still the light increased in intensity—and then, and then, the most exquisite sense of release . . . a great final orgasm, a giving up of the whole being. . . .[1]

It is interesting that Maugham likens death to "a great final orgasm," the ultimate orgasm, since the word "ecstasy," from the Greek, means literally "standing out of

[1] Garson Kanin, *Remembering Mr. Maugham* (London, Hamish Hamilton, 1966).

one's self." We say that a thrilling musical passage "sends" us, or that "I was *beside myself*" with joy. These linguistic clues suggest a universal, age-old awareness of out-of-the-bodiness. And, as the supreme out-of-the-body experience, death is the ultimate ecstasy.

The great psychiatrist, Dr. C. G. Jung, whose life was a stream of dazzling supernormal experiences, once died and returned and always looked back on that happening as the profoundest reality he had known.

Jung relates that, early in 1944, after a minor accident, he had a heart attack and slipped over the edge of death. While being revived with camphor injections and oxygen, he participated in a drama which was awe-inspiring in its power and scope.

He seemed to be transported far above the earth and to hang suspended in space. Below, he saw the globe, "bathed in a gloriously blue light." The continents unrolled beneath him like a multihued carpet.

Off to one side Jung saw a magnificent temple, and he was about to enter an illuminated room therein where he would meet, he knew, "all those to whom I belonged in reality." He felt that "the whole phantasmagoria of terrestrial existence was stripped from me," and that soon he would receive an answer to the riddle of existence.

At that moment an image floated up from Europe. It was Jung's doctor who told him he had no right to leave and must return at once. Thereupon the vision faded.

Significantly, when Jung realized he was back in his physical body his feeling was not relief or joy but—and this is typical in such cases—profound disappointment, even gloom.

"The whole world struck me as a prison," he confessed, and a painful nostalgia for the place he had visited haunted him for three weeks.

Of his mini-death, Jung, after much reflection, said: "I would never have imagined that any such experience was possible. It was not a product of imagination. The visions and experiences were utterly real; there was nothing subjective about them; they all had the quality of absolute objectivity. . . .

"I can describe the experience only as the ecstasy of a non-temporal state in which present, past and future are one. . . . 'This is eternal bliss,' I thought. 'This cannot be described; it is far too wonderful.' " [2]

Out-of-the-bodiness does not always project the experiencer into another world. Sometimes the trip is very short —to the ceiling.

In one case, also reported by Jung, a woman hemorrhaged severely after childbirth and, just before sinking into an inky void, was aware that the nurse rushed to the bedside to take her pulse.

The next thing she was aware of was that she was *looking down* from a point near the ceiling and able to observe everything going on in the room below. She saw herself lying in bed, ghastly (or perhaps "ghostly" would be better) pale, her eyes closed. Beside her stood the nurse. The doctor, apparently frantic, paced up and down the room. Her mother and her husband came in and looked at her with great distress on their faces.

All this time, the woman herself was aware that behind her loomed a wonderful landscape glowing with vibrant colors, especially an emerald green meadow which shimmered in pale yellow sunlight.

Then, with no sense of time having passed, the woman

[2] C. G. Jung, *Memories, Dreams, Reflections* (New York, New York Books, 1963).

awakened in the hospital bed and was told by the nurse that she had been unconscious for half an hour. The next day, when the woman good-naturedly criticized the doctor to the nurse for his "hysterical" pacing up and down beside the bed, the nurse, incredulous, at first denied that the patient could have any knowledge of this since she had been unconscious at the time, but then admitted that it was true. And so were the other things the woman had seen, such as her mother and husband standing over her with anxious looks.[3]

These experiences raise a number of questions: Is out-of-the bodiness pathological? Why the variations in what the out-of-the-body experiencers perceived? Do such experiences only occur in medical crises, or can they happen when people are living quiet, ordinary lives? Can they be induced at will?

First, consider the question of whether such experiences are morbid.

There is a psychological phenomenon known as *autoscopy,* or sometimes *heautoscopia,* described as "seeing yourself without a mirror." This uncanny experience, shared by such people as Goethe, Dostoevsky, and Freud, involves perceiving a projection of one's own body image, either as an hallucination, an illusion, or a vivid fantasy. There is nothing supernormal about autoscopy, nor abnormal. It is not necessarily pathological, although, because of its uncanniness, the experience "is usually accompanied by great anxiety."[4]

Are out-of-the-body experiences merely a form of autoscopic hallucination?

[3] C. G. Jung, *The Interpretation of Nature and the Psyche* (New York, Pantheon Books, 1955).
[4] Irving Beiber, M.D., "Body Image . . . ," in *Encyclopedia of Aberrations* (New York, The Citadel Press, 1965).

Dr. Nandor Fodor, the distinguished psychoanalyst and psychical researcher, did not think so. He suggested that even subjectively it may be possible to distinguish between fantasy experiences and those which appear to be more. Fantasies of being out of the body, he noted, usually feature the center of consciousness in the *physical* body—the person is aware that he is lying on the bed watching his other self float around the room. However, classic out-of-the-body experiences, such as the ones we have considered, feature the center of consciousness *not* in the physical body but in the other self separated from it. It is this other self which observes the physical form lying on the bed.

Moreover, an autoscopic hallucination, the psychiatrists tell us, is generally accompanied by great anxiety, whereas, as we have seen, true out-of-the-bodiness is accompanied by feelings of tranquillity, bliss, illumination, ecstasy.

The evidence strongly suggests, then, that out-of-the-body experiences are different in *kind*, and not merely in *degree*, from those with which the psychiatrist is generally familiar.

Another question is why, if the experience has some element of objective reality, those who have it see different scenes. One person describes a biblical-like city made of light; another has the sensation of flying out of, and back into, his body without seeing anything; another floats in space high above the earth and contemplates a shining temple which awaits him; while another gets only as far as the ceiling of her room. Why these differences if the experience in each case is not merely subjective?

There are several things which can be said. One is that what people see no doubt depends on how long they are out of the body. The longer the experience, the farther, presumably, the out-of-the-body traveler can go (although spatial metaphors, it seems, are misleading). Another factor is that what people see on these excursions could well be determined, to a great extent, by their beliefs and expectations, even though these may be largely unconscious. This does not in any sense invalidate the objectivity of the experience. After all, two people may visit London, one an Anglophile and the other an Anglophobe, and bring back reports so disparate as to make it appear that they had visited different cities. A crude analogy but apt nonetheless. Psychologists know that even our most ordinary perceptions are shaped, to a greater extent than most of us realize, by the complex emotions we bring to the act of perceiving.

Moreover, consider that two visitors to our planet would take back what appeared to be descriptions of different worlds if one landed in the jungles of central Africa and the other in Antarctica.

It may also well be true that perceptions of the out-of-the-body environment vary because of the nature of that environment. This leads to such questions as where people go when they go out of their body; and do they have another body besides the physical? These important issues will be considered later in this chapter when we examine the exact significance of out-of-bodiness for belief in survival after death.

For the moment let us grant that the variations in descriptions brought back by out-of-the-body travelers are not necessarily incompatible with the idea that what such travelers see is objectively real.

The question whether out-of-the-bodiness is experienced by people other than the dying, and whether the phenomenon may be deliberately induced, leads to some very significant data.

Many people, it seems, experience out-of-the-body excursions often, if not routinely. In some cases the experience is wholly spontaneous and can no more be controlled than sneezing, except that, like a sneeze, it sometimes can be suppressed. That is, if the person feels himself going out of his body, and doesn't want to go, he can apply a sort of mental brake and abort take-off.

In other cases people claim to have brought their out-of-bodiness under fully conscious control. There is considerable evidence that this is possible, some of it obtained in the scientific laboratory.

Dr. Charles Tart, of the psychology department at the University of California in Davis, has published startling results of experiments he conducted involving out-of-the-body experience. His prize subject was a young woman, identified only as Miss Z, who claimed to have had out-of-the-body experiences two to four times a week throughout most of her life. During a typical such experience she would awaken at night to find herself near the ceiling and her body lying on the bed below. Only once or twice, it seems, did she ever venture farther than the ceiling, and then not far—certainly not into any "astral" plane.

Miss Z claimed to have a high measure of control over these experiences. Also, she said that on seven consecutive nights, as an experiment, she drew a random number out of a cardboard box which contained slips of paper bearing numbers from 1 to 10; she put the slip of paper beside her bed, without looking at it, and later, while out of the body, would try to read the number. She claimed to have gotten the correct number each time.

Dr. Tart put these claims to the test.

His laboratory was divided into two sections. One was a sleeping room for Miss Z, equipped with instruments for recording changes in her brainwaves, heartbeat, breathing, and circulation. The other section was a room in which Dr. Tart could monitor the changes in Miss Z's vital functions and keep her under visual observation, if he chose, through a window in the wall.

Miss Z had wires about two feet long connecting her to the instruments. Any attempt on her part to do more than merely turn over in bed or sit up would pull out the wires and, as Dr. Tart put it, cause "all hell to break loose" on the instruments.

Some five-and-a-half feet above Miss Z's head was a shelf. Above that, on the wall, hung a clock. Each night of the experiment Dr. Tart wrote a random five-digit number on a piece of paper and placed it on the shelf, beyond the subject's range of vision. The task assigned to Miss Z was to project herself out of her body and read the number on the slip of paper, and the time.

On the first three nights of the experiment nothing much happened. Miss Z reported getting part-way out of her body—as a knife may be pulled partly out of its scabbard, presumably—but nothing significant showed up on the instruments. Miss Z generated the usual delta waves of deep sleep, and showed the rapid eye movements (REM) associated with dreaming, but that was about all. Once she did say she had glimpsed the clock and thought the time was three-fifteen, but this was not particularly evidential.

However, on the fourth night things livened up considerably. At 6:04 A.M., reported Dr. Tart, Miss Z awakened and called out that the target number was 25132—which was correct. Not only that, in the moments before she awakened—that is, during the time she presumably was out of her body—Dr. Tart's instruments gave some unusual readings. Miss Z's EEG showed a bizarre pattern which Dr. William Dement, one of the world's foremost dreamologists, confirmed could not be classified as belonging to any of the known stages of drowsiness or sleep, nor to the REM stage of dreaming.[5]

There was, then, a significant correlation between, (a) the subject's giving of the correct number, and (b) the more or less simultaneous appearance of an unclassifiable pattern on the EEG. Was this pattern characteristic of out-of-the-bodiness? Will it someday be so identified, just as other EEG patterns are associated with certain states of consciousness?

Recent experiments with another voluntary out-of-the-body traveler have been reported by Dr. Karlis Osis, director of research of the American Society for Psychical Research, New York.

The subject, Ingo Swann, an artist and writer who lives in New York, calls what he does the ability to "exteriorize." He claims to be able to project himself into unfamiliar environments—another room, say, where he has never been—and to describe what he sees.

Dr. Osis said that the central hypothesis of his research is that man has an "ecsomatic (literally, out of the body) aspect capable of operating independently of and away from the physical body."

In a typical experiment the subject, Ingo Swann, sits quietly in a semidark room, attached to a polygraph (located in an adjoining room) which monitors his brain-

---

[5] Charles Tart, *Journal of the American Society for Psychical Research* (January, 1968).

waves, heart rate, breathing, and other physiological processes.

The task assigned the subject is to "exteriorize" himself to a point in space from which he can describe several target objects located on a shelf suspended two feet from the ceiling of the room, beyond his normal range of vision. These objects have been chosen for "possessing strong form and color," in Dr. Osis's words, so as to be well-defined and readily recognizable—e.g., an umbrella, a black scissors case, an apple. Ingo Swann is asked to describe the objects and to specify the particular angle or perspective from which he is observing them. (This last detail is to test the hypothesis that the out-of-the-body traveler's center of perception has a location in space which differs from his physical location. In other words, if he is really up near the ceiling, his descriptions of the objects should betray that fact.)

After eight experiments an outsider evaluated the results by blind judging—that is, he was asked to match up Ingo Swann's descriptions with the correct objects without knowing which target each description was meant for. The judge correctly matched all eight sessions, indicating that in each of them Ingo Swann's descriptions corresponded to the targets on that occasion.

"The likelihood of getting 8 out of 8 by chance," said Dr. Osis, "is approximately 1 in 40,000." [6]

Apparently Ingo Swann's brain wave activity showed high-amplitude voltage changes during the out-of-the-body periods but Dr. Osis cautioned that any definite

[6] Karlis Osis, Ph.D., "New A.S.P.R. Research of Out-of-the-Body Experiences," *Newsletter of American Society for Psychical Research*, No. 14 (Summer, 1972).

statements about this aspect of the phenomenon would be premature. Research designed to probe such areas continues.

A crucial question looms up: Are out-of-the-body experiences instances of merely a form of ESP—so-called "traveling clairvoyance"—or has the exteriorizer (to use Ingo Swann's term) an actual body, different from the usual physical body, during the period he is exteriorized?

There are two aspects to this question, namely, does the exteriorizer perceive himself with a body; and do others ever perceive him with a body?

We have seen, in the last chapter, that a person may project a mental image of himself by telepathy into another's consciousness. Is it possible that some of these apparitions are actually out-of-the-body projections and not merely mental images? Or is it, rather, the case that when an out-of-the-body traveler is seen by somebody what is perceived is merely a telepathic hallucination? Is or is not some real, quasimaterial form projected?

There is at least one test to distinguish a hallucination from an objective appearance: Can it be photographed? Since a camera cannot be hallucinated, a likeness of an appearer, if it is captured on photographic film, cannot have been merely a telepathic image. For something to be able to influence the emulsion on the film it must scatter light; that is to say, have at least quasiphysical properties.

There are cases in which the exteriorized form has been photographed, though none that I know of under experimental conditions. Elsewhere, I have described a photograph, now hanging in the provincial parliament buildings in Victoria, British Columbia, which shows the ethereal likeness of a man who allegedly was not present when the picture was taken.[7]

Charles Good, a member of British Columbia's first Legislative Council, apparently was at home sick in bed, comatose according to some reports, when the council met on January 13, 1865; yet his face—strangely transparent, "ghostly"—appears in the official photograph.

Belief in a counterpart body has a long history. Traditionally, certain conditions are said to facilitate or trigger the separation of the duplicate body from the physical—trance, deep sleep, physical or psychological shock, severe illness (as in Charles Good's case), or the imminence of death.

The second body is called, traditionally, by various names—the astral self, the etheric form, the psychic double, the spiritual body.

This double—a perfect counterpart of the physical body, supposedly, except for blemishes—is said to be composed of a subtle, attenuated, or rarefied matter. It is reputed to be capable of interpenetrating the physical body, and other material objects, as a gas penetrates fabric; or, better, as a neutrino (the "ghost particle" of physics, which has an electrical charge but no mass) passes through lead.

What evidence is there, besides some ambiguous photographs, for the existence of a human double?

Scientific evidence comes, interestingly enough, from the Soviet Union where parapsychologists have turned up startling clues to what they call the "energy body," the

[7] Allen Spraggett, *The Unexplained* (New York, New American Library, 1967).

"biological plasma body," or simply the "bioplasma body."

This entity is described by the Soviet scientists in terms similar to those used by clairvoyants, who have always claimed to be able to see, surrounding and intermeshing with the physical body, another body of light and colors. (Psychics call this iridescent, pulsing mass, visible to them around a human being, the "aura" or "auric field.")

Soviet researchers, using a technique known as "Kirlian photography" (after its discoverers, Semyon and Valentina Kirlian), which consists of photographing a person or other living organism in a high frequency radiation field, have obtained astonishing pictures of this counterpart body, like a carnival of colored lights, engulfing the physical form. The second body is not merely electrical activity, say the Soviet researchers, though it behaves like electricity, but is composed of a new, unknown form of energy.[8]

For us, the crucial question is: Does this counterpart body survive the death of the physical?

If it does survive, this fact has great bearing on the question of the *nature* of the next world.

The Soviet researchers, operating as they must within the context of a Marxist, materialistic ideology, tread lightly on the issue of life after death. However, they do describe how, at the death of the organism, the undulating mass of energy which makes up the second body withdraws from the physical, as helium escapes from a punctured balloon, and swims off into space. And where then? Soviet scientists do not, officially at least, pursue the postmortem destiny of this energy body.

[8] Sheila Ostrander and Lynn Shroeder, *Psychic Discoveries Behind the Iron Curtain* (Englewood Cliffs, New Jersey, Prentice-Hall, Inc., 1970).

But we can pursue that destiny, though from here on things must be frankly speculative. Let us make a hypothesis and examine what, if any, evidence there is for it.

The hypothesis is that at death the second body, serving as the continuing vehicle of consciousness, moves into another world, dimension of existence, or domain of nature (whichever term one prefers), where the individual as a self-conscious entity continues his spiritual evolution.

Let us, then, from here on call this human double the *theta* body—"theta" being the first letter of the Greek word for "death."

If our hypothesis is valid, certain things follow.

One is that since the theta body, being quasimaterial, has dimensions, the next world must, in some sense, have dimensions, as well as location. But if so, where is it located?

My suggestion is that the next world takes the form of a parallel universe. The theoretical concept of parallel, or interpenetrating, universes is perfectly respectable among physicists. Here is what a distinguished scientist, the chairman of a department in the physical sciences at a large American university, told me:

> It is possible for there to be other forms of matter which obey different quantum rules, in which the electron spin, let us say, is plus and minus two-thirds instead of plus and minus a half; and this matter could not interact with our present matter. It is perfectly possible, then, to have parallel universes, or interpenetrating universes, where the matter of one would not interact with that of the other. But under some triggering—such as a mental triggering of some sort—you could have momentary interaction.

Such a parallel universe would not necessarily be anywhere else than where we are now; it could occupy exactly the same space. And yet, under "normal" circumstances, we would have no contact with that other world or its inhabitants, nor they with us. Under a mental triggering, however (the desire, on either side, to communicate?), such contact might be possible.

A prominent British scientist also has discussed co-existing worlds:

> Perhaps there do indeed exist universes interpenetrating with ours; perhaps of a high complexity; perhaps containing their own forms of awareness; constructed out of other particles and interactions than those we know now, but awaiting discovery through some common but elusive interaction which we have yet to spot.[9]

Though these scientists were talking about the concept of parallel worlds in general, not specifically an after-death one (though the first quoted does personally believe in a postmortem state), their descriptions fit admirably our hypothesis of a next world suitable for the theta body; a world intermediate between matter and non-matter; a world with which communication would be possible, if at all, only under certain conditions, or, on the other hand, with which communication could be regular, or frequent, though normally undetected.

There is significant evidence from certain mediumistic communications tending to support such a concept of the next world, and we will look at it in this chapter. However, let us pursue a little further the question of what the next world is like.

[9] Denys H. Wilkinson, F.R.S., "Matter and Sub-Matter," *The Listener* (July 31, 1960).

The postulate of a theta body outflanks those critics who have argued, rightly or wrongly, that unembodied survival of personal identity is impossible.[10] However, let us for a moment consider the concept of total bodilessness for possible insights which may enrich our understanding of survival.

Philosopher H. H. Price, professor emeritus at the University of Oxford, argues that bodiless existence after death, the critics notwithstanding, is quite conceivable.

"If the after-death personality is something wholly immaterial," he asks, "can there be any sort of other world at all?"

He goes on to answer the question: "It seems to me that there can be. We could think of it as a kind of dream world." [11]

In dreams, Price points out, we have bodies; and we move in a world of images which are as real, while we are dreaming, as any physical environment. So, after death our unembodied consciousness could create a dream-world of images as real as the material world.

Would everybody's after-death dream-world be totally subjective and private? Not necessarily, says Price.

From what we know of telepathy and clairvoyance it is altogether plausible, he suggests, that different "dreamers" could interact and by telepathic collaboration create a collective image-world as "public" (in the sense of being perceived by more than one person) as our environment is here and now. (After all, if a roomful of people, under

---

[10] Terence Penehum, *Survival and Disembodied Existence* (London, Routledge & Kegan Paul, 1970).

[11] H. H. Price, "What Kind of Next World?" in *Man's Concern with Death* (London, Hodder & Stoughton, 1968).

hypnosis, were hallucinating exactly the same scene would not that scene be for them indistinguishable from physical reality?)

The sort of postmortem dream world, for some people perhaps, nightmare-world, that Price postulates finds echoes in Milton:

> The mind is its own place, and in itself
> Can make a Heaven of Hell, a Hell of Heaven . . .

(Price offers the intriguing suggestion that the purpose of our present life is "to provide us with a stock of memories out of which an image world may be constructed when we are dead.")

My own feeling is that the next world is intermediate between mind and matter, the material and the immaterial. It combines, in a concept more plausible than either one is separately, the view of the afterlife as a material world and that of it as a dreamlike state of mere images.

The core of human consciousness, the psyche, the soul, the spirit, the essence of each of us, which expresses itself through a physical body here and a theta body hereafter, is, I believe, a nonphysical entity. It is timeless and spaceless; immeasurable, imperceptible; pure being. As Nandor Fodor put it: "The soul is something we cannot conceive of in shape or form at all—something which we cannot even understand. It is an intangible, immaterial, invisible part of us. . . ." [12]

In the present world of time and space, this core of

[12] Spraggett, *The Unexplained.*

consciousness manifests through a physical body which is perfectly at home in this environment. After death, where a different set of rules prevail, the same consciousness manifests through a theta body which is adapted to those rules.

The next world, being composed of matter subtler than this, is malleable by mind; mental states are translated more or less directly into objective reality. The power of the mind to mold matter, glimpsed here only in fugitive, elusive flashes of psychokinesis, in the next world comes to full blossom. There, in very fact, "the world is my idea."

The concept of like-minded discarnate personalities telepathically pooling their thoughts and thereby creating a collective world for themselves is quite plausible. And since personalities seek their own level of spiritual development, there would be many next worlds corresponding, perhaps, to the "many mansions" of the Gospel.

I am suggesting, then, a next world where the basic "stuff" is intermediate between mind and matter (one could even imagine it having its own fundamental particle called, perhaps, a "psychon"); where human beings live on and express themselves through theta bodies; where people's mental states are objectivised; where individuals gravitate to the plane, dimension, or sphere which corresponds to their level of consciousness or spiritual evolution; where individuals share, through telepathic interplay, the same world-within-a-world; and finally, where individuals continue to progress to "higher" planes as they spiritually evolve.

Arthur Ford, one of the greatest mediums in history, made a number of trance statements about the after-death environment which support this view of it. Once, Ford's control, Fletcher, speaking for a purported discarnate, said:

> He was and still is your only son, because he hasn't moved to some other planet, he hasn't gone to some other place. In the spiritual body he has simply come into another dimension but it's a world that interpenetrates yours. It is like, if you stop to think, that this room and all the atmosphere around you right now is full of people and full of voices just as real as yours. They are living people, living and speaking, but until you turn on the television set you can't see and hear them, can you? Well, that's the way we are. It's just another dimension, another wave length, so to speak. . . . [13]

In another trance utterance, Ford-Fletcher talked about how, in the next world, thought is translated into things.

> Over here we have clothes, but they are not clothes that we put on. They are clothes—well, if I decide I want to look like a certain time or certain period, I think that, and it's sort of a radiation of light from our body. . . . It's fashioned in the style of dress we want. . . . [14]

A woman who had an out-of-the-body experience during an operation reported entering a world such as Fletcher seemed to be describing.

Mrs. Geraldine Tuke, an Englishwoman, after going under general anesthesia saw her body being wheeled into the operating theater, then that scene faded and another opened to her gaze.

[13] Allen Spraggett with William Rauscher, *Arthur Ford: The Man Who Talked with the Dead* (New York, New American Library, 1973).

[14] Spraggett with Rauscher, *Arthur Ford: The Man Who Talked with the Dead* (New York, New American Library, 1973).

A dead niece, Eileen, met Mrs. Tuke, and showed her the home she lived in on the other side. Eileen explained that though the rooms in her house were fairly permanent, because she was at present satisfied with them, the contents were not.

The things she made lasted as long as she wanted them. If she became tired of one, it dissolved and she made something better.

Mrs. Tuke asked her niece if she could "make" something.

"She told me to give a clear thought of what I wanted," Mrs. Tuke said.

"I pictured a vase of lovely shape and color. There was in my hands a substance which I should call a lump of vibration. I could see the thought picture clearly. My hands put the picture into the substance.

"It was not solid but putting the thought into it made it so. It was living and full of vitality." [15]

This image of a world of thought congealed into objects does not sound as bizarre today as it would have 50 years ago before the advent of atomic physics. Compare the concept of objects as thought-forms and this description by a scientist of what, behind the appearance of solidity, a physical thing really is:

> . . . It is a whirling mass of atoms which keep a formation because they are continually held in shape by a coordinating "field." The sand grains that in a dust storm permit us to see the shape of the wind vortex are not that vortex but its manifestation. . . . The wind vortex, when it leaves the desert and goes over the mountain,

[15] *Quarterly Review of the Churches' Fellowship for Psychical and Spiritual Studies* (Autumn, 1972).

drops its sand grains. The vortex is still there but has become invisible. . . .[16]

If, as Bishop Berkeley surmised, material things are indeed thoughts which "subsist in the mind of some Eternal Spirit"—a concept which may represent only a slight rephrasing, really, of the view that physical objects are whirling electrons within an invisible organizing field—then the notion of a next world where things are thoughts is not inherently unreasonable.

It would explain why out-of-the-body travelers give somewhat different descriptions of the landscape in that next world.

All in all, the evidence presented in this chapter, for me, strongly points to the existence of a next world like the one we have hypothesized.

But there is still further evidence, which strengthens the proposition that you will never die, to consider.

[16] Gerald Heard, "Don't We Survive Death?" *The First Occult Review Reader*, Bernard J. Hurwood, ed. (New York, Award Books, 1968).

CHAPTER 5

The Evidence from Threshold Experiences Just Before Death

On January 12, 1924, a woman (identified only as Mrs. B) was dying in the Mothers' Hospital, Clapton, England. Her sister, Vida by name, had died the previous December 25, but because of her own condition Mrs. B had not been told.

However, as Mrs. B was sinking into a final coma she suddenly exclaimed: "I can see my father." And then, in a tone of puzzlement: "He has Vida with him. Vida is with him!"

The woman died shortly after.

This case, reported by Sir William Barrett, one of the founders of the Society for Psychical Research,[1] belongs to a category which older psychical investigators used to call "Peak in Darien" experiences (from a book of that title, by Miss E. P. Cobbe, about such cases).

The distinguishing mark of this type of experience is that the dying person "sees," waiting to welcome him on the other side, a loved one or friend whom he did not know was dead. The vision is accompanied by the appropriate reaction—surprise, incredulity, shock—at seeing the one not known to be dead.

[1] William Barrett, *Death-Bed Visions* (London, Methuen, 1926).

Such a case was reported by Natalie Kalmus, pioneer developer of technicolor in motion pictures. Mrs. Kalmus's sister, Eleanor, was dying and Natalie was at her bedside.

Suddenly the sister pushed herself up in bed, almost to a sitting position.

"Natalie," she murmured, "there are so many of them. There's Fred—and Ruth—what's she doing here? Oh, I know!"

Mrs. Kalmus said that at these words an electric shock went through her. The dying woman had mentioned *Ruth*. But Ruth was her cousin who had died suddenly the week before, and Eleanor had not been told of her death.

"It's so confusing. There are so many of them," the woman exclaimed.

Then she sank back and died.[2]

Threshold experiences (taking place, that is, at the threshold of death) provide additional compelling evidence that human personality vanquishes time and space, and their dark progeny, decay and death.

Leslie Weatherhead tells the case of a woman described as "very difficult, bad-tempered, and irreligious" who, though gravely ill, refused to see a clergyman and raged against her fate. Then she died—or appeared to die. However, after receiving a stimulant, she revived. What happened then astounded the nurse who had come to know this woman very well.

"She opened her eyes," recalled the nurse, "and said slowly, in a voice I had never heard before and solemn beyond description: 'I have been dead and all my dying's

[2] *Coronet* (April, 1949).

done. I have seen the angels and they are more beautiful than I can tell.' " [3]

From then, said the nurse, until her death 24 hours later, this formerly bitter, resentful patient was gentle, long-suffering, and blissfully serene.

What particularly astounded her, confessed the nurse, was the fact that a woman with no faith in an after-life saw "angels" and died in perfect confidence that they were waiting for her. The patient's mind-set would appear to have been antagonistic to such a hallucination (although one could always argue, I suppose, that her *unconscious* expectations may have been quite different from those which were conscious).

The question of mind-set is important in evaluating hallucinatory experiences. If we assume, at the moment for the sake of argument (though we will see shortly the assumption is a valid one), that the dying often experience pleasant and reassuring hallucinations, can this be explained in terms of majority mind-set?

Actually, there is evidence that, on the contrary, what the psychologists call a "negative expectancy set" is the majority attitude today toward hallucinations. Most people, in other words, do not expect ever to see a hallucination and may not even believe that such a thing is possible.

Some skeptics are tempted to attribute every apparitional experience to a lamentable, apparently almost universal tendency for people to hallucinate at the drop of a hat. To hear these skeptics, the average person is hallucination-prone, especially where anything ghostly or otherwordly is concerned.

[3] Leslie Weatherhead, *Why Do Men Suffer?* (Toronto, McClelland & Stewart, Ltd., 1936).

But is this true? Are people today apt to perceive mystical things at the slightest provocation?

Some members of the Cambridge Society for Psychical Research wanted to test how prone people were to see apparitions and such. One of them, A. D. Cornell, masqueraded as a traditional ghost, the sort reputed to prowl the drafty corridors of English castles. Draped in white, he disported himself in a lighted churchyard in view of a busy street. Many passersby noticed him but subsequent questioning revealed that none took him for an apparition. One man speculated that what he had seen could have been a polar bear, perhaps escaped from the zoo. But a ghost? Evidently that possibility had not occurred to him.

Even more significantly, in his ghost outfit Cornell glided twice across the screen during a movie and 32 percent—almost a third—of the audience did not even notice him. The rest came up with some colorful and ingenious guesses about his identity but not a single person mentioned an apparition.[4]

This experiment suggests that in contemporary British —and probably North American—society there is a rather marked bias against seeing apparitions. Why, then, should many of the dying suddenly begin hallucinating? Or, in fact, do they? How common—and how evidential— are deathbed visions anyway?

There is a traditional folk belief that when a person approaches death his deceased relatives or friends draw near to form a sort of welcoming committee to the next world. In a day when many doubt that there is a next world,

[4] A. D. Cornell, "Further Experiments in Apparitional Observation," *Journal of the American Society for Psychical Research*, No. 706 (1960).

such a belief, and the stories told to support it, tend to be discredited as mere superstition or, at most, examples of delirious fantasies induced by disease or drugs.

However, a respected parapsychologist, Dr. Karlis Osis, when he was research director for the Parapsychology Foundation, New York, did a careful, definitive study of contemporary threshold experiences.[5] He found startling evidence which tends to corroborate the traditional lore about deathbed visions.

In any such study there are two main parts: the raw data, and the evaluation and interpretation of that data. To get his data Dr. Osis sent out 10,000 questionnaires to physicians and nurses across the United States requesting detailed information about their observations of "terminal patients." He received 640 replies describing more than 35,000 deathbed cases. Osis followed up many of these by phone interviews and correspondence.

The survey shot down many popular misconceptions about dying.

For one thing, said Dr. Osis, the common view that as death draws closer fear grows stronger is not true. Fear does not appear to be a dominant emotion among the dying.

Indeed, according to the survey, many terminal patients experience a mood of euphoria, even elation. In some cases the dying person displays emotions so elevated that they could fairly be described as "exaltation."

This predeath ecstasy appears to be unrelated to such factors as the patient's sex, education, social status, race, or particular religious persuasion (although a *strong* re-

[5] Karlis Osis, *Deathbed Observations by Physicians and Nurses* (New York, Parapsychology Foundation, 1961).

ligious faith, whatever its content—contrasted with mere nominal allegiance to a specific creed—does seem to have a positive significance).

Even more interesting from the scientific point of view is Osis's discovery that the terminally ill patient often sees visions or hallucinations, which tend to take certain forms. Sometimes these are of traditional religious images —heaven, golden cities, angels—and sometimes they are scenes of "indescribable beauty and brilliant colors," not unlike the best trips reported by users of psychedelic drugs.

Yet, contrary to what one might expect, these deathbed visionaries are not drugged or delirious but perfectly sane and lucid. In most cases the patient's perception of his actual environment remained normal and intact while he was seeing the vision. Delirious or drugged people, by contrast, are disoriented and tend to misperceive everything in a phantasmagoric way, as in one of those distorting mirrors at a carnival.

Most common of all among dying persons, Osis found, are visions of dead loved ones, usually close relatives. In some instances these proved to be "Peak in Darien" cases in which the hallucinated relative was not known by the visionary to be dead.

Dr. Osis estimated that hallucinations among lucid terminal patients are 10 times as common as among healthy people in the general population, and he wondered why this should be so.

"Does this fact," he asks, "mirror another aspect of reality?"

Are the dying, in other words, seeing something that is really there though normally imperceptible? Is there something about the immediacy of death that sensitizes the mind to sights and sounds usually unseen and unheard?

Several interesting distinctions showed up in the study. One was between the hallucinations of nonterminal and terminal patients. The nonterminal patients—those who were ill but not in danger of dying—hallucinated either living people or religious imagery more or less in keeping with their personal faith. The terminal patients, however, saw almost exclusively visions of the dead.

There was a significant difference, too, between the visions of those apparently terminal patients who recovered and those who died. Those who died saw people they loved who said they had come to receive the newcomer into the next world. Those who recovered, on the other hand, often saw relatives who *refused* to take them into the next world.

"One patient," said Dr. Osis, "reported that his dead father told him: 'No, not now, Willy, go back.'"

Were these differing experiences shaped by the patients' having become aware through extrasensory perception of whether or not they would die (the ESP impression being translated into the form of a vision), or were the experiences objective reality? Did the spirits in some cases actually welcome the dying and, in the others, urge them to wait?

The theory that hallucinations of the dying are not merely subjective fantasies is strengthened by the fact that some of them have collectively perceived. A few such cases are reported by Osis.

One nurse recounted seeing a hallucination of a dying patient's deceased sister at the same time that the patient did. The apparition stood by the side of the bed, clearly visible for several moments to both women. The nurse wrote a description of the experience in her note-book.

The threshold experiences which made the deepest impression on attending doctors and nurses were those in which the patients reached the suburbs of death and returned, often briefly, with reports of transcendent visions. Osis calls this "seeing the beyond" and noted that "these revived patients intensely desired death, to return to the experience of indescribable beauty and peace connected with dying."

This kind of experience is distinguished from the out-of-the-body phenomenon by being less structured, less sharply defined. Whereas the out-of-the-body traveler has a definite sense of being separated from his physical self, of being caught up either into a particular location in space or into another world altogether, the person who "sees the beyond" does not feel that he has gone anywhere but, rather, that a curtain has been drawn aside to permit him a glimpse of what lies behind it.

"Why did you bring me back?" one revived terminal patient who had peered behind that curtain reproached his doctor. "Let me go back. It's so beautiful over there."

Dr. Osis concluded that his study confirmed two hypotheses of previous students of deathbed visions; namely, that terminal patients frequently hallucinate and nearly always dead loved ones or friends; and that the express purpose of these visitations is to aid the patient's transition into postmortem existence.

Though cautious in his interpretation of the data, Osis points out that while other theories may explain certain features of these threshold experiences, the survival hypothesis covers them all.

Long regarded as merely subjective emotion, threshold

experiences prove, rather, to be a strong link in the chain of evidence supporting survival.

Now let us consider some more evidence that human beings not only survive death but use extraordinary ways, when necessary presumably, to indicate their survival.

CHAPTER 6

The Evidence from Death
Coincidences and Signs of Intention

Thomas Alva Edison, the great inventor, died at 3:24 A.M.,
Sunday, October 18, 1931.

In his laboratory office three minutes after his death a
big 30-day wall clock stopped. Three of Edison's top associates noticed that their clocks also stopped at 3:24 A.M.

There seemed to be no ordinary explanation for these
four instances of clock-stopping. The night watchman
at the Edison Laboratory where the inventor had his
office, John Flanagan, told Edison's son that he had not
stopped the clock himself. And the three executives
attested that there was no reason they were aware of why
their clocks should have stopped at the same time as
Thomas Edison's death.[1]

Jung would have called this an example of synchronicity, or "meaningful coincidence"—the pairing of events
in a way that has meaning but cannot be ascribed to a
normal cause-and-effect relationship.[2]

Some of Edison's friends and associates wondered

[1] Berthold Eric Schwarz, M.D., "The Telepathic Hypothesis and
Genius: A Note on Thomas Alva Edison," *Corrective Psychiatry*,
Vol. 13, No. 1 (January, 1967).
[2] C. G. Jung, *Synchronicity: An Acausal Connecting Principle*
(New York, Pantheon Books, 1955).

about the possibility of a more-than-coincidental connection between the inventor's death and the stopping of the four clocks in view of the words of the popular song, "Grandfather's Clock," which Edison had recorded on both cylinders and discs (his inventions) and of which he was very fond. The lyrics read:

> It [the clock] was bought on the morn
> Of the day he was born
> And was always his treasure and pride;
> But it stopped short, never to go again
> When the old man died.

There was an added link between Edison and the song: Since his early manhood his employees and associates were in the habit of calling him "The Old Man."

Moreover, Edison was known to have had a profound interest and belief in psychic phenomena, and even tried to construct a machine capable of communicating with the dead. The inventor is said to have told an associate that he hoped the device would pick up communications from some "outer sphere—some message from somewhere, somehow, that wasn't the earth plane . . ." [3]

It is difficult, surely, to attribute the stopping of four different clocks at the time of Thomas Edison's death to mere chance. Telekinesis seems more probable—that is, the direct action of psychic force to produce a physical effect. But *whose* psychic force—Edison's or that of his associates? Did the discarnate inventor provide the energy which stopped the clocks or did it emerge from the associates' unconscious minds?

[3] Schwarz, "The Telepathic Hypothesis and Genius: A Note on Thomas Alva Edison."

Before we try to reach a conclusion on this question, let's look at some further examples of what can be called death coincidences.

Actually, there are numerous instances of clocks stopping, and sometimes starting, coincidentally with a person's death. Occasionally it has been claimed explicitly in mediumistic communications that the deceased person caused the odd behavior of the clock as a "sign" of his continued existence.

When Professor James Hyslop, president of the American Society for Psychical Research, died, his daughter's watch stopped at the same moment. His secretary, Gertrude Tubby, without knowing about the watch-stopping incident, had a sitting with a medium, identified only as Mrs. Saunders, at which Hyslop purportedly communicated and said that he had affected his daughter's watch as a sign of his presence.[4]

In 1966 Terry Allen of Indio, California, went to Viet Nam with the United States Army. He arranged for his girlfriend to buy, with his money, a wall clock for his mother.

The clock ticked away uneventfully for five months; then, on May 5, 1967, at 2:10 P.M., it inexplicably stopped. A few days later a telegram arrived saying that Private First Class Terry J. Allen of the Ninth Infantry Division had been killed on patrol in the Mekong Delta.

The young man's death occurred on the date—and, so far as his bereaved parents were able to determine, at the moment—that the gift clock stopped.[5]

One of Dr. Louisa Rhine's informants tells a similar

---

[4] Gertrude Tubby, *James H. Hyslop: His Book, a Cross Reference Book* (York, Pennsylvania, 1929).

[5] "The Clock Struck Two," *Fate* (December, 1970).

story. A clock over a hundred years old, which had belonged to the informant's father and to his mother before him, sat on a mantel in the front hall of her Chicago home. The woman's parents lived with her.

"The day of Mother's death in 1952 the clock stopped at the exact time of her passing," the woman said. "I rewound the clock and the next day it stopped at that exact time. The clock uses more than 24 hours to run down before stopping, so that would eliminate its second stopping, at that exact time, being due merely to its needing rewinding." [6]

A case in which a timepiece inexplicably *started* is reported by psychiatrist Berthold Schwarz who, at approximately 2:30 P.M., Sunday, October 14, 1962, was called to the apartment of his friend, Jacques Romano, a gifted clairvoyant, to pronounce him dead. Romano's pocket watch had stopped at eight-forty, possibly indicating the time of death. Since Schwarz had seen many peculiar phenomena in Romano's presence, he took special note of the stopped watch. A few minutes later, when he looked at the watch again, it spontaneously had started running and was ticking merrily away. [7]

I have had a personal experience with a clock which seemed to show a mind of its own.

My father died on Monday, January 6, 1964. It was 4:30 A.M. when the hospital phoned with the news that he had passed away a short time before.

From my father's apartment I brought home an old alarm clock which my parents had used as a regular time-

[6] Louisa E. Rhine, *ESP in Life and Lab* (New York, Collier Books, 1967).
[7] Schwarz, "The Telepathic Hypothesis and Genius: A Note on Thomas Alva Edison."

piece for some 20 years, though I could not recall their ever having made use of the alarm on it. This clock sat on a shelf in our kitchen, behaving itself, for several days.

Then, on Sunday night—one week after my father's death—the clock suddenly started buzzing, waking my wife and me from a sound sleep. We discovered that the alarm—which I hadn't touched—was set at four-thirty. It was the time that the news of my father's death had come to us exactly a week earlier.

As my wife said: "Who would set an alarm clock for a time like that?"

A certain type of matter-of-fact skeptic, I'm aware, is exasperated by stories such as these. "If the dead really communicate," he demands, "why do they perform such silly, pointless antics?"

But are they silly, pointless antics?

Though no verbal message is communicated, such manifestations can be plausibly interpreted as "signs"—vivid and dramatic ones—that a deceased personality is still in existence and able, however inadequately, perhaps, to manifest his presence. In most of these cases there is a strong, even inescapable sense of *intention*. The manifestations do not appear to be random, haphazard, but seem to have a logic of their own.

It may be that after-death conditions are such that sometimes the deceased can only manifest in ways which seem to us odd or even bizarre. If a miner, trapped below ground in a cave-in, can indicate his survival to those on the surface only by tapping with a wrench on a pipe, he accomplishes his purpose, however limited the form of communication may be.

Often, too, there is a deeper meaning in these telekinetic manifestations than may at first appear. They have significant symbolic overtones, apparently reflecting the same kind of logic of the unconscious that manifests in dreams.

Consider the many cases involving clocks. A clock, when you think about it, is not at all a bad symbol of mortality—of the remorseless, one-way movement of time which carries us all ever closer to death. The stopping of a clock, at or very near the moment of a person's death, could be interpreted as signifying entrance into a dimension where time is no more.

The inexplicable starting of a watch which apparently had stopped at the moment of the owner's death—as in the case of Jacques Romano—could symbolize that life, which seemingly has come to a stop, actually continues.

Let's look at some further cases and seek the possible inner logic in each, the evidence of intention and meaning which might escape mere casual consideration.

Sometimes—and these are unusually dramatic cases—the telekinetic effect follows a deliberate attempt at contacting the dead person.

A California man, two nights after his wife's death, felt her presence strongly and said aloud: "If you are here and can hear me, give me a sign." Instantly, a decorative metal chariot with two heavy horses crashed to the floor from its position atop a chime clock on the mantle where it had sat undisturbed for 12 years.[8]

In this case, we do not know if the metal chariot had a particular association with the dead woman—whether she had bought it herself, perhaps, or especially cherished it for some sentimental reason—but investigation might well

[8] Henry W. Pierce, *Science Looks at ESP* (New York, New American Library, 1970).

have proven this to be so. At any rate, when such a manifestation occurs, as though in direct response to a spoken request, the impression of apparent *intention* is heightened.

Next to clocks, perhaps the most common type of death coincidence involves lights—lights inexplicably going on, or off, or flickering, or, occasionally, flaring to preternatural brightness. This is not surprising in view of the powerful symbolism which light and darkness hold for most of us. Such figures of speech as: "I suddenly saw the light," "Her face lit up," or "It was like going from darkness to light," betray these profound emotional overtones and undertones.

Dr. S. Ralph Harlow, a clergyman who for years taught philosophy at Smith College, tells how he and his wife were discussing a very close friend named Helen on the night of her death (that is, she had died during that day). Before going to sleep, Harlow said mentally: "Helen, if you can give us any sign of your conscious survival, won't you please do so?"

Both he and his wife were awakened in the middle of the night by a bright beam of light playing on the bedroom wall. It was projected by an old, rusty, two cell flashlight whose batteries Harlow knew to be corroded and which he had put aside as useless some two months before.

"Now," said Harlow, "it was ablaze with light."

He got out of bed and switched off the flashlight. When he tried to put it on again it refused to light. He flicked the rusty switch off and on a number of times, and shook the flashlight, but to no avail—no light.

The next night, Harlow again tried the flashlight, and once more it refused to light. Before going to sleep, he and his wife mentally attempted to contact their dead friend, Helen, and asked, if indeed it had been she, to give them a sign again.

At two o'clock they were awakened by the flashlight blazing even more brightly than on the previous night.[9]

In this case the light phenomenon was not synchronous with the death of the person but followed attempts to evoke a sign of her continued existence.

In another instance, the noteworthy behavior of an electric light coincided with death. An elderly widow and her adult daughter were reading one night in their respective beds on opposite sides of the same room when the mother's, but not the daughter's light went off.

Both took special notice of this otherwise unexceptional incident because they had just been talking about a friend, seriously ill in the hospital, for whom they were greatly concerned. The sick friend, named Philip, had helped the widow through a financial crisis following her husband's death and had shown great consideration for both her and her daughter.

When the light went off, the daughter looked at the clock beside her bed. It said ten-thirty. Three minutes later the light came back on.

Word arrived soon after that their friend Philip had died in the hospital at ten-thirty.[10]

Dr. Harlow, who recounted the experience with the flashlight, reported another, even more startling, incident which occurred after the death of his wife.

[9] S. Ralph Harlow, *A Life After Death* (New York, Doubleday & Co., 1967).

[10] Louisa E. Rhine, *Mind Over Matter* (New York, Macmillan, 1972).

Writing in *Gateway* (formerly the publication of Spiritual Frontiers Fellowship), the clergyman said he and wife had agreed that whichever one died first would try to communicate a key word to the other as a sign of his or her continuing life. The key word was "light."

Two days after his wife's death, Harlow got a letter from a woman he did not know saying that she had received automatic writing which purported to come from his wife. In the first part of the letter, the key word, "light," was used four times. But that was not all.

The letter instructed Harlow, at ten o'clock on the evening of the day he received the letter, to go to the cupboard in his home where the china was kept and his wife would try to give a sign of her presence. He invited a friend to be present as a witness.

That evening, Harlow and the friend went to the cupboard and turned on a light. Immediately it went off and on—12 times, by actual count. The two men tested the bulb; it was not loose. There was no loose fuse. None of the other lights in the house acted at all unusually.

Can anyone honestly dismiss an incident such as this as trivial, or pointless? Can anyone fail to understand or appreciate how evidential such an experience is for the one to whom it happens?

All the objections in the world that the means of communication seem unworthy of an intelligent person does not demolish the experience. And who are we to lay down terms as to how the dead must communicate?

The light phenomenon was doubly significant in this case, as evidence of intention, because it not only followed explicit instructions from the deceased person who was attempting to manifest her presence but also paralleled the agreed-upon key word which was to serve as a special guarantee of authenticity.

Who could fail to grasp the import of this nonverbal message: "I've found the light. There *is* light, not darkness. Keep following the light!"

Sometimes post-mortem telekenesis adopts the symbolism of growth and blossoming, as though life were a flower which death does not cut down after all.

My friend, Dr. Nandor Fodor, the distinguished psychoanalyst and parapsychologist, died on May 17, 1964. Immediately before and after his death a number of unusual, apparently telekinetic signs occurred in the penthouse apartment which he and his wife shared in Manhattan.

One of them concerned roses.

"On our terrace," said Mrs. Fodor, "there are flowers. The climbing roses usually last four days, then lose their petals and new buds form. But (after my husband's death) the roses, about 150 of them, bloomed at once and lasted for seven weeks.

"For that period of time no rose dropped a petal. Then one day they all withered together. I cut them off and as I did so I asked for just one rose. I got it one week later—just one rose, which also lasted seven weeks." [11]

A dramatic incident concerning flowers happened to the famous author Taylor Caldwell.

As her husband, Marcus Reback, lay dying he held her hand and murmured: "If there is life after death I will come back and give you a sign."

He died on August 13, 1970, and was buried three days later.

[11] Amarya Fodor, "Does Dr. Nandor Communicate?" *Fate* (January, 1965).

A few hours after the funeral, Taylor Caldwell heard her housekeeper calling to her in an excited voice. In the yard, the grieving author saw, blooming for the first time since it had been planted 21 years before, a shrub of resurrection lilies.

She and her husband frequently had joked about the poor showing this particular shrub had made over the years, and he had once quipped: "You can't prove the resurrection by these lilies."

Now, on the day of his funeral, that shrub was gloriously, fragrantly, inexplicably in full radiant bloom.[12]

Again, there is a manifest logic to this incident, as with the previous one concerning Nandor Fodor. Mrs. Fodor had asked for one rose, for a sign of her husband's ongoing life, and a week later one rose bloomed and remained for an extraordinarily long time. And a sorrowing Taylor Caldwell, on the day of her husband's burial, was confronted by the unprecedented spectacle of a shrub, about whose unproductivity her husband had jested, in dazzling white bloom. And the name—could anything be more meaningful, more appropriate; again, more indicative, in the circumstances, of intention, than *resurrection lilies?*

Sometimes people speak of "shattering" evidence, and there are occasions on which these telekinetic signs have provided just *that*.

S. Ralph Harlow, previously mentioned in this chapter, had a sister, Anna, who was highly gifted with psychic powers and to whom he was devoted. She died suddenly in 1925.

After the funeral services, Harlow returned to his office

---

[12] Taylor Caldwell, *Ladies Home Journal* (October, 1972).

at Smith College where he was teaching philosophy. He had a conference scheduled with a student and decided to proceed with it, hoping that it would distract him from his grief. The conference, significantly perhaps, dealt with a course on William James's treatise, *Varieties of Religious Experience.*

As Harlow and the student sat at the big desk in his office on that October day, he toyed with a large glass inkwell and thought about his sister.

"Since I've just come from a funeral," he said to the student, "perhaps we can approach the varieties of religious experience by my telling you something about the religious experiences of my sister Anna."

At that instant, as he pronounced his sister's name, there was a loud report and the inkwell on Harlow's desk split in two. The fracture was clean, and halved the inkwell into parts of virtually equal size.

The student, trembling, rose and hurriedly excused herself, saying: "I'm afraid to stay here."

Later, Harlow asked a colleague at Smith, a physicist, about the phenomenon. After examining the halves, the physicist said that only two things could have caused such a spontaneous fracture in solid glass—a sudden, marked change in temperature (which there had not been) or some powerful vibration.

"You know, like a boat's whistle cracking a glacier," the physicist remarked.[13]

Is it possible, Harlow wondered, that there had indeed been a sudden, powerful vibration—not from a boat whistle (there was no boat nearby) but from the other side? When mediums speak of "vibrations" do they speak more truly than perhaps even they know?

[13] Harlow, *A Life After Death.*

Again, we are confronted by a set of circumstances which seem inexplicable by chance alone. A woman, known to be highly psychic, dies. Her brother, who shared her psychic interest, returns from her funeral. While thinking of her he toys with an inkwell on his desk. A moment later, at the precise instant he mentions her name, the inkwell shatters into perfect halves—a phenomenon which, from the standpoint of physics, is unaccountable under the circumstances.

Can anyone really believe that this chain of events adds up, as certain skeptics would argue, to precisely zero? Can anyone believe that the inkwell just *happened* to shatter at the moment that the sister's name was mentioned?

And, too, can anyone fail to perceive in this incident an apparent inner meaning? Can anyone genuinely doubt that, in the particular circumstances, the incident appears to be indeed a *sign*, an evidence of intention, a visible manifestation of an invisible presence?

There are some cases of telekinesis apparently linked with the dead in which the phenomena are subtle, complex, and of an exceedingly dramatic kind—so much so that the evidence of intention becomes almost irresistibly convincing. Here are two cases which fit this category.

The Reverend Canon Robert Lewis, rector of St. Mary's Episcopal Church in Haddon Heights, New Jersey, who was mentioned in a previous chapter, is deeply interested in psychical research and has had several extraordinarily evidential experiences. One of them concerned his grandmother's photograph.

The grandmother, who lived near Scranton, Pennsylvania, was Welsh-born and a very devout Baptist.

"My grandmother raised me, pretty much," Canon Lewis said, "and always thought that I was the image of her husband, my grandfather, who died three years before I was born."

Lewis remembered his grandmother as a deeply religious, emotional person who, like many women, generally expressed great happiness by weeping. Whenever her grandson did something she was especially proud of, she wept for joy.

"The Welsh are very psychic too," said Canon Lewis, "and so was my grandmother."

When Bob Lewis decided to become a priest and entered the Episcopal Divinity School in Philadelphia, his grandmother was overjoyed and, as usual, wept. Sadly, she died of a brain hemorrhage two years before he completed his studies and was ordained.

But she may not have missed her grandson's ordination after all. This is how Canon Lewis finishes the story:

In my room at the seminary I had a picture of my grandmother sitting on a chest of drawers.

During my senior year of study I had to take my canonical exams before the bishop and his examining chaplain. This is both a written and an oral test. If I passed it, I would be ordained. So it was a very important test indeed for me.

It was the end of April when I took the canonical exams and after the test the bishop informed me that I had passed. On the way back to the seminary I had an emotional time thinking how happy and proud my grandmother would have been, knowing that I was to be ordained. But she had been dead for two years.

When I got back to the seminary I went to my room and glanced at my grandmother's picture. To my astonishment it was soaking wet. Moisture had streaked my grandmother's face. The picture inside the glass of the frame, was wet—so wet that the back of the picture was beginning to buckle. There was a small pool of water under the picture where it had run out onto the chest of drawers.

Several seminarians came into my room and saw the wet photo and so did one of my professors. No one had an explanation.

I felt that my grandmother knew about my exams and that she had reacted in the way most typical for her— she cried.

Canon Lewis's story is corroborated by another priest, the Reverend Canon William V. Rauscher, who was a fellow seminarian and witnessed the discovery of the "weeping" picture.

I took my canonical exams, in a different diocese, the same day Bob Lewis took his [says Canon Rauscher] and, wanting to compare results with him, I went to his room in St. Paul's house at the seminary and rested in an easy chair waiting for his return.

I dozed and it wasn't until I heard the door open that I awoke. Bob entered looking very tired. He sat down and told me about the exams and how, during the bus ride from his diocese, he had thought about his grandmother. He mentioned how pleased she would have been to know that he would become a priest.

He got up and went over to the dresser to take off his tie. A look of confusion came over his face as he glanced at his grandmother's picture. He turned to me angrily and asked if someone were playing a joke. I said no, what did he mean. Had anyone been in his room? As far as I knew the house was empty except for myself and one other student, who had not been in the room and, moreover, was definitely not the joking kind.

> As we examined the grandmother's picture we found that it was soaked with water inside the glass. Even the back of the picture, which was made of a dyed imitation velvet, had faded and run, streaking the color. . . .

Canon Rauscher adds the significant detail that when the picture dried "the area about the face remained raised, as though the water had run from the face downward. The picture remains the same to this day."

This is indeed a curious case. Ruling out trickery—which, considering the character of the two witnesses, is unthinkable—what possible explanation can there be?

Not only do we have a physical effect of a peculiarly impressive sort—one which seems inexplicable by any normal means—but it corresponds to a marked personal trait of the deceased person purportedly giving the sign.

The incident, in other words, has an inner logic, a psychological consistency. Flashing a light on and off, or shattering a glass, presumably would not have been particularly in character for Canon Lewis's grandmother, but weeping? That was precisely the emotional reaction to have been expected in the circumstances.

But how—by what conceivable mechanism—could this telekinetic effect have been accomplished?

Dr. Nandor Fodor developed, from his psychoanalytic experience, a hypothesis for such cases of weeping photographs (of which there are more than a few). Fodor called the parapsychological process involved "at-oneness," and described it as being the exact opposite of the familiar psychological mechanism known as "identification."

The latter is what occurs when an individual unconsciously, or partially so, behaves, or imagines himself behaving, as if he were another person to whom he had a profound emotional tie. An example is the case of a medieval mystic who, praying long before the image of the crucified Christ, *identifies* so intensely with the image that he develops physical stigmata. These are marks or lesions corresponding to the traditional wounds of Christ. In some cases, the lesions open only on Fridays—the traditional day of Christ's crucifixion—and blood oozes from them. Psychoanalysts regard them as *hysterical* lesions— physical effects produced by the mind's influence on the body (analogous to the blister formed on a hypnotized subject by touching his skin with a pencil while telling him it is a red-hot poker).

Now, at-oneness, as Fodor described it to me in conversation, is the reverse of identification; instead of a person taking upon himself the characteristics of a statue or a picture—as the stigmatist takes on the wounds of the crucified Christ-image—he projects *his* characteristics onto the statue or picture.

Fodor believed that in genuine cases of weeping paintings of the Virgin Mary, for example—and he said he had investigated some which seemed authentic—the tears were actually those of someone in the household. Somehow, sorrow, grief or anguish which could not be expressed normally was transposed, unconsciously, onto the painting. It was not the inanimate Virgin weeping but someone in the house whose tears could find no other outlet and who, if the anguish did not express itself, might actually have died of it.

The relevance of Fodor's remarks to the case of Canon Lewis's grandmother is evident. If living human beings can effect the phenomenon of at-oneness, can the dead also? Is it not conceivable that a grandmother, determined to communicate a sign of her continuing existence and joy to one left behind, could project onto a photograph the visible manifestation of what she deeply felt?

The alternative is that the telekinetic force came from Canon Lewis's own unconscious mind. However, this counterhypothesis is only more plausible than that of discarnate intervention, I submit, if the possibility of survival is rejected. On the basis of the evidence presented in previous chapters, however, survival is at least highly probable, and, that being the case, one has to decide which is the more likely—that Canon Lewis unwittingly caused the photograph to "weep," or that his still-existing grandmother, full of love and joy and more psychic than ever, accomplished this dramatic effect knowing it would be received by the one for whom it was intended as an utterly characteristic, endearing, and cherished sign of eternal life.

It is simpler, I suggest, and more in keeping with the data, to believe that the discarnate grandmother made her presence known.

If the critic asks why the grandmother did not choose some other form of communication—a direct, disembodied voice speaking from the middle of the room, say—I have no answer, although there are several possible ones. Perhaps the dead cannot choose their mode of communication; perhaps there are constraints, limitations upon them of which we know nothing. Or perhaps it is easier, somehow, for them to produce telekinesis than an auditory manifestation. If a medium, unconscious or otherwise, is needed for the production of any psychic effect—that is, a living person from whom some or all of the necessary energy is drawn—it may be that more people have telekinetic potential than other kinds.

Certain unusual occurrences followed my own mother's death—events which I had the opportunity to discuss in detail with Dr. Fodor and which he said were among the most impressive evidence of contact by the dead, with apparent intention, that he had encountered.

My mother was 64 years old when, after a long illness, her heart failed on January 4, 1960.

At the time I was a theological student and pastor of three rural churches, living with my wife and children some 300 miles from my parents' home. I received the sad news by phone from my brother.

My relationship with my mother was ambivalent, as it is between most mothers and sons, I suppose. But if friction and strain were there, so was love. Her death came as a shock to me—a more painful one, it turned out, than I was prepared for.

Six weeks after her death I went into my study one night and shut the door. I had decided to try an experiment. Perhaps my state of mind could be characterized best by Emily Dickinson's lines:

> . . . not precisely knowing
> And not precisely knowing not.

In this mood I sat in the dark trying to project my thoughts into the great unknown. I thought, is my mother still alive out there? Where *is* out there? If she is alive, is she aware of me now? Can I reach her?

Presently I said aloud: "If you are there and can communicate with me in some way, please do it."

My words sounded strangely hollow. I sat in the darkness for a long time—waiting. For what? I didn't know. But in those moments I felt a great tenderness.

Later, getting ready for bed, I told my wife, Marion,

who was already half-asleep, what I had done. She mumbled a reply and turned over. As soon as I was in bed I fell into a deep dreamless sleep.

In the morning when I went to the wardrobe to get my trousers I found my belt tied into a series of knots. I was annoyed and muttered something like, "For heaven's sake, who did this?" Although it took considerable effort to undo the knots nothing clicked in my mind. It didn't occur to me that there might be a connection between the unusual state of my belt and the experiment of the night before.

I mentioned the knotted belt to my wife. She shrugged it off as another of my personal eccentricities.

"You must have done it yourself." she said—and there the matter dropped.

The next morning when I went to the wardrobe I found the belt in the same condition as the day before, but worse. This time the knots in the black leather belt were so tight I couldn't untie them, although I plucked at them furiously.

Thoroughly exasperated, I exploded: "What in blazes is going on here? Who on earth *did* this?"

My wife chuckled. "Maybe it wasn't anybody on earth," she said lightly. "Could've been your mother."

But a moment later she stopped chuckling. When she took her dress from the wardrobe she found that *her* belt was now a series of knots—identical to those in mine.

We sat down and seriously discussed this crazy belt-knotting. I knew I hadn't done it—not consciously, anyway—and Marion insisted she wasn't playing a practical joke.

Could one of us have done it while sleepwalking? Possibly, we decided, but not likely. In six years of marriage neither of us had ever known the other to talk in his sleep, much less walk.

What about the children? We ruled them out. Stephen was five and Alanna was only two. Even if one of them could have opened the wardrobe, no small child could have twisted the resistant belts into such tight knots.

Was it, then, my mother?

Neither my wife nor I are spiritualists but we were open-minded about the possibility that my mother might have reached us from the other side—especially in view of my experiment.

For the next week nothing odd happened. We continued to ponder the significance of what had taken place. If it really were my mother, I thought, why did she choose so bizarre a method of communicating? (At the time I was not so aware of the large number of similiar cases.) Twisting belts into knots! How crazy can you get?

On the other hand, I reasoned, what if conditions in the afterlife are such that the dead can communicate only in odd ways? Perhaps, too, the belt-knotting had a deeper significance than was immediately apparent.

Maybe the manifestations were genuinely paranormal, all right, but triggered by power released from my own or my wife's unconscious mind. Perhaps I had wanted something to happen after my experiment and unconciously made it happen. Was I—unawares—a poltergeist?

A week later, on impulse, I repeated my experiment. I told Marion what I was going to do. Shutting myself in my study as before I beamed my thoughts into the vast abyss, holding the image of my mother in my mind's eye.

"If you were trying to contact us," I said quietly, "please let us know. Do it again."

The next morning our belts were undisturbed—but at

breakfast Marion and I were not. We got embroiled in a domestic spat. When things got hot I jumped to my feet saying, "I'm going to drive into the country and get a little peace and quiet."

"Well, you're not going to take the car," my wife retorted (she's a tigress when provoked) and snatched the car keys away from me. Being no match for her in a wrestling bout, I didn't try to recover the keys but took the spare car key from her purse and headed for the garage.

When I got in the car I reached into my right trouser pocket where I had put the key a moment before, but now it wasn't there. A strange sensation went through me. My mother? Was it possible?

I got out of the car and searched for that key, covering the driveway on my hands and knees, but there was no sign of it. When I told Marion what had happened she joined me in the search. No luck.

"Look," I said, "If this has anything to do with my mother—I don't know whether it has or not but I did try that contact last night—it's very important that we be absolutely certain about what happens next.

"I want to be sure in the future that we're not tempted to say we only imagined what happened, or that it didn't really happen the way we thought it did."

"Well," said Marion, "what shall we do?"

"To begin with, let's make absolutely sure that the car key isn't anywhere on me."

There and then we made an exhaustive search of my clothing. I undressed and Marion went through my pockets, the lining of my trousers and shirts, my socks and shoes. No key.

"All right," I said as I got dressed. "No matter what happens now we know that key wasn't on me."

"What are we trying to prove?" Marion asked.

"I don't know," I admitted. "I just have a feeling that my mother may be involved here. If so, some funny things are apt to happen, and if they do I want to be sure we're clear about them."

That was all I could say about my state of mind. It was difficult to describe what I felt—a sort of subliminal sense of something impending. What, I couldn't say or imagine, but the feeling was very real to me.

At that moment the doorbell rang and it proved to be a young man, a neighbor, who wanted me, as the local pastor, to give him a reference. He hoped to go to the United States and enlist in the Army there. (We were in Canada, of course.)

Inviting him into the living room I sat down in an armchair and he took a chair across from me. Idly, I put my hand in my right trouser pocket.

A shock went up my arm. *The key was back in my pocket!*

I got that boy out of the house as fast as I could and broke the news to Marion. She almost collapsed.

"You've *got* to be joking," she said.

I handed her the key, but one of us fumbled and it fell to the floor with a clatter. Marion bent to pick it up. It was the same key, all right.

My wife and I looked at each other, both thinking the same thing: Mother?

Some time later I spent a memorable afternoon discussing these incidents with Dr. Nandor Fodor. He seemed fascinated and asked numerous questions.

"Are you or your wife subject to unaccountable lapses of memory?" he asked. "Do you walk or talk in your sleep?"

I said no.

"Are you readily hypnotizable? Has either of you ever been hypnotized?"

I replied that although I had used hypnosis I seemed to be a refractory subject myself and the same was true of my wife.

I knew, of course, what Fodor was driving at. He was trying to determine, as he said, if we were subject to automatism—that is sometimes quite complicated behavior performed involuntarily and leaving no conscious recollection. People who are subject to such minor "fugues" almost invariably have a history of sleepwalking, unexplained lapses of memory, sometimes a marked inclination to daydream or an unusual susceptibility to suggestion.

"In your case," said Dr. Fodor, "this doesn't seem to apply."

"What about hallucination?" I asked.

"It's possible, of course," he replied. "But consider what it would have involved. You felt the knots in your belt, you handled the key and heard it drop to the floor. This means the hallucination had tactile and auditory elements as well as visual.

"And since your wife shared it, it was a collective hallucination. From my clinical experience I can assure you that while collective hallucinations do happen they are rare, exceedingly rare."

Dr. Fodor suggested that for the moment we assume that the experiences were genuinely paranormal and try to discover what significance they might hold.

"I'm interested in the symbolism of knots," he said. "Were there any nautical associations in your mother's family, a sea captain perhaps?"

I couldn't think of any.

"Then why knots?" Fodor's brow furrowed. "Was your mother eccentric in any way?"

I smiled. "As a matter of fact my wife and I agreed that tying belts into knots was just the kind of thing you might expect her to do. My mother was—how shall I put it —a little, well, twisted."

"Twisted?" Fodor's eyebrows shot up.

She was cockney, I explained, born in east London within the sound of Bow Bells. As such she had a wide streak of drollery, of the "character," in her.

"Then twisting belts would not be *out* of character for her?" Fodor said.

I agreed. Not out of character at all.

"And the key." Fodor continued. "It might have symbolized the answer that opens the mystery of life after death. As if your mother were saying: 'Here, I give you the key.'"

I raised an objection. Subsequent attempts I made to contact my mother were unsuccessful. If my mother actually had communicated, why didn't she respond to these later attempts?

"Why should she?" Fodor replied "Would you? After giving you such evidence she may have felt that if it didn't convince you nothing would."

Summing up, Dr. Fodor concluded that he felt the most likely explanation of the case was that my mother *had* contacted me. In fact, he went even further.

He said that in his 30 years of research these experiences were perhaps the most persuasive instances of alleged contact by the dead, with evident intent, that he had encountered.

CHAPTER 7

The Evidence from Memories
of Previous Lives

With most forms of evidence for human survival, the problem is to prove that someone who is unquestionably dead still exists. But can the problem be approached from the opposite direction—that is, to prove that somebody who is unquestionably alive once died?

This new approach is the contribution of reincarnation research to solving the riddle of survival. Such research is based on the study of living people to determine, if possible, whether or not they lived before on earth.

A Dutch portrait painter, who now lives in New York, was born Henrietta Roos but married a man named Weisz whom she subsequently divorced. Though in Holland divorced women usually resume their maiden name, Mrs. Weisz found her married name unaccountably appealing to her and, as a compromise, called herself Mrs. Weisz-Roos.

During a time in Paris, where she was studying painting, she had a peculiar experience in which an audible voice awakened her from sleep and told her to take up her brush. In a kind of psychic thrall, only half aware of what she was doing, the woman got up from bed and painted. The next morning she was astounded to find that she had done an exquisite miniature portrait of a young woman.

She took the painting to a clairvoyant, who, in trance, told her that she had been guided in painting it by Goya, the great Spanish artist, who wanted to express his appreciation to her for having once saved his life. In her previous incarnation, said the psychic, Mrs. Weisz-Roos had given the painter shelter when he was driven into exile.

At the time Mrs. Weisz-Roos had read nothing about Goya but that same evening she looked up a biography of the painter and discovered that during his exile he had lived in the home of a woman named Leocadia Weisz.[1]

There are numerous cases—Dr. Ian Stevenson, alumni professor of psychiatry at the University of Virginia medical school, has collected 600 of them, many of which he has personally authenticated—of individuals who give striking evidence of one sort or another that they lived previously on earth. And if they once lived—a hundred or 200 years ago—they must have died, and been reborn. Evidence for reincarnation is evidence for human survival of death.

The word "reincarnation" means literally to take another flesh, another body. It is the theory or belief that humans pass through a series of earthly lifetimes on their way to ultimate perfection. (The superstition that people may be reborn as lower animals is not, strictly speaking, reincarnation but metempsychosis, or the transmigration of souls.)

The doctrine is fundamental to Hinduism and Bud-

[1] Ian Stevenson, "The Evidence for Survival from Claimed Memories of Former Incarnations," *Journal of the American Society for Psychical Research* (April and July, 1960).

dhism. In these eastern religions the wheel of rebirth is called, in Sanskrit, *samsara*. The law of moral cause and effect which governs reincarnation ("Whatsoever a man soweth, that shall he also reap") is called *karma*. And the ultimate goal of the process of rebirth is, for the Buddhist, *nirvana* (literally "a blowing out," as a candle is extinguished), and for the Hindu, absorption into Brahman, the primordial sea of pure being from which all things flow and to which they return.

In the eastern faiths, authorities differ on what the state of nirvana, or merger with Brahman, really means. Some say the individual blends into Being Itself as the dew drop slips into the silver sea. This is interpreted as the end of *individual* existence but not of existence. The individual note of music exists in a symphony but its existence is meaningful only in its relationship to all other notes in the symphony, not as a separate entity. So it is with the individual, say the Hindus, when he becomes one note in the cosmic symphony of Being.

Buddhism, for its part, teaches depersonalization as the goal of rebirth. The doctrine of *anatta* (literally, "no soul") says that man is but a bundle of *skandahs*, or perceptions, moving across the screen of consciousness. There is, for the purist in Buddhism, no abiding central ego. What, then, is reborn? It is the bundle of karmic debts which the individual has accumulated in his earth life. When one candle is lit from another, ask the Buddhist sages, what is passed on? Is it the same flame or a different one? Thus, there is a continuity in earth lives but no constant ego or self serving as the vehicle of that continuity.

However, Ian Stevenson, who is a deep student of Buddhist thought, feels, as a result of his own intensive reincarnation research—much of it involving cases in Buddhist countries—that the doctrine of anatta or "no soul" is, as he put it to me, "getting very shaky." There must be, he insists, some structure, some entity, which persists from one earthly lifetime to the next. Otherwise, he holds, there could be no reincarnation, for the very word clearly implies that *something*, once in a physical body, has taken up another physical body.

But what is that *something?*

C. J. Ducasse suggested a distinction between what he designated the *personality* of the human being and the *individuality*. Personality derives from the Greek word "persona," the ritual mask worn by the players in ancient Greek drama. The personality, then, in Ducasse's usage, is a mask which the individuality puts on and which varies completely from one earthly life to the next.

What, precisely, is the difference between the two? Personality most of us can grasp, but of what does our individuality consist?

Well, think of yourself, the same bundle of genetic endowments with which you were born into this life, as you might be now if you had been born somewhere other than where you were born—somewhere radically different, say Communist China. You have, remember, the identical natural endowment—same I.Q. (or whatever you want to call your innate intellectual potential), temperament, and biochemistry. Born and raised in China, however, identical genes notwithstanding, you would now be a very different personality.

Your religion, moral values, philosophy of life, world view, social relationships—these, and virtually everything else about you, would be dissimilar to what they are now. The personality, in the sense in which we are using the word here, is shaped by the particular social and cultural forces which play upon it. Yet if you were now a communist Chinese, behind that personality would lurk the very same individuality which wears your present personality.

You, then—the individuality made up of the unique bundle of your congenital endowments—have worn many personas, many masks, on your long pilgrimage through time and space. Or so Ducasse and other believers in reincarnation contend.

Many people have found the doctrine of rebirth attractive because it offers an answer to the inequities of life— why one man is born a prince and another a pauper, why one is born into this world with every blessing, it seems, while others appear to be damned into the world.

Our present condition, says the reincarnation philosophy, is due entirely to ourselves. We are the cause, as well as the result, of ourselves, of what we were and thought and did in previous lives. We are the sum total of effects flowing from causes which we ourselves created.

The law of karma, as understood by reincarnationists, is not in any sense a principle of punishment; it is impersonal, like the law of gravity. If you jump out of a high window and break your leg, has the law of gravity punished you? Rather, when you break the law you break yourself.

In Christian terms, karma is the law of harvest—"whatsoever a man soweth," says the New Testament, "that shall he also reap."

This means, of course, that karma is positive as well as negative. Sow figs and you reap figs; sow thistles and you reap thorns. Sow kindness and you reap it in the next life if not in this; sow hate and you reap it—usually in this life as well as the next.

The ethical doctrine of karma is a demanding one of total personal responsibility. There are no excuses, no alibis, no I-wish-I-had-done-better escape clauses. We are what we are because we were what we were.

However, all is not grim fatality. Western seers, such as Edgar Cayce and Arthur Ford, taught that there is "a law of Grace" which can neutralize bad karma. The law of Grace operates on the premise that you may extinguish within yourself the element of character which generated the negative karma; if, for example, you pay off the debt you incurred in a past life, through culpably taking lives, by saving them this time around, the baleful effects for you are dispersed, dissipated, dissolved.

Does reincarnation conflict with the concept of survival which emerges from the previous chapters—the concept of a parallel next world from which, at times, people are able to communicate through mediums or other manifestations?

There is no contradiction between the two. Indeed, many—perhaps most—of the great mediums of our time have believed in reincarnation. Certainly Cayce did (reincarnation was central to his philosophy), Ford did, and so did Uvani and Abdul Latif, the two main trance personalities of Eileen Garrett, another famous medium.

Between earthly lifetimes, say these mediums, there are intermissions or interludes spent in the next world. During these interludes, which apparently may be as long as several earthly centuries or as short as even a few hours, the individual is supposed to distill, out of the memories of his incarnation just ended, the essence of its meaning for him. When he has assimilated this meaning, understood the significance of his past life, what he learned and what he failed to learn, where he succeeded and where he did not, how he grew or stood still or regressed, then he decides when, where, and how to plunge back into time and space to continue his spiritual pilgrimage.

Many find this concept of a steadily unfolding spirituality and growth over a succession of lives stirring, challenging, sublime. Others do not, preferring, once they have served their time on earth, not to come back for another stretch. But presumably the law of karma is universal and reincarnation applies to all, and equally. Yet, we are told, those who come into what appear to be tragic, even wretched, earth situations do so not against their will but as a free acceptance of a fate which they have decreed for themselves.

And always, at the end of the pilgrimage, be it relatively long or short, looms the transcendent radiance of that perfection which awaits, at last, all of journeying mankind.

What is the evidence—the hard, empirical evidence— for reincarnation? There are many strands which, interwoven, comprise a strong and convincing case for it.

Prodigies may be explained by reincarnation—extraordinarily gifted children who, like Mozart, compose at 5 or, like the French poet Minou Drouet, write at age nine a verse which begins: "My heart is an empty boat whose harbor is nowhere."

The fact of child prodigies, though suggestive, does not in itself require reincarnation as an explanation. Yet, such inexplicable talents, skills, or facilities often appear to be karmic. So, too, may be other not readily explainable traits—such as a strong predilection for, or conversely a fear of, some place, person, or object; or even strange physical characteristics. Consider some cases.

Joan Grant, a noted British author, had a lifelong

allergy and phobia to feathers which resisted conventional treatment. In an altered state of consciousness she "remembered" an experience in a previous life when vultures swooped down to attack her; this recall ended the allergy and phobia to feathers. The significant fact here is the disappearance of her psychological and physical symptoms, which argues strongly that what she recalled was an actual memory and not merely fantasy. What happened to her would be analogous to the experience of a patient who, during psychoanalysis, "abreacts" a traumatic incident from his early childhood and thereafter is free of his chronic neck pain, for instance, or sinusitis or asthma. The remission of a symptom, particularly one of long standing, strongly suggests that true recollection is going on, since a mere fantasy would not be likely to have such marked effect.

In a slightly different case, San Francisco psychiatrist Blanche Baker reported that a patient of hers recalled, during deep analysis, being stabbed in a previous existence. The next day Dr. Baker noted an area of erythema (redness, inflamation) on the patient's back at the spot where he remembered the knife going in.

The clinical significance of the erythema is that similar somatic effects are often noticed in psychiatric practice when an adult patient, recalling being whipped early in life, let us say, develops actual lesions such as were caused by the whipping. In some cases these weals bleed. Similarly, rope burns have been known to appear on the wrists of a man who vividly relived the experience of having been brutally tied some years before.[2] (Of course,

[2] Stevenson, "The Evidence for Survival from Claimed Memories of Former Incarnations."

physical marks, such as blisters, can be produced by hypnotic suggestion, so the appearance of skin lesions during apparent recall of events in this or a previous life does not guarantee that the memory is genuine. However, taking into consideration other evidence, such physical exteriorizing of a claimed memory can constitute corroboration that the purported events did indeed happen.)

Many of Ian Stevenson's cases involve idiosyncratic, even bizarre, birthmarks which may well be rebirth marks.

A boy who claimed to have been shot in World War I bore on his body two birthmarks strikingly similar to scars of bullet wounds.[3]

A boy in India named Ravi claimed to remember being stabbed to death when incarnated as a boy named Munna. Besides other extremely evidential features in the case, Ravi had a birthmark on his throat which resembled the scar of a knife wound; the child, Munna, it was discovered, had had his throat slit.[4]

An Alaskan named Corliss Chotkin has claimed from early childhood to be his own great-uncle reborn. The dead man, Victor Vincent by name, had predicted that he would come back with identifying birthmarks matching two surgical scars on his body—one from an eye operation, the other from a lung puncture. Young Corliss has two such birthmarks, and the one on his back clearly corresponds to a lung puncture, showing what appear to be stitch marks.[5]

[3] Stevenson, "The Evidence for Survival from Claimed Memories of Former Incarnations."

[4] Ian Stevenson, *Twenty Cases Suggestive of Reincarnation* (New York, American Society for Psychical Research, 1966).

[5] Stevenson, *Twenty Cases Suggestive of Reincarnation.*

There are also unpublished cases which Ian Stevenson has told me about. He found a man in a southern Turkish village who claims to remember having been hanged as a horse thief; around his neck he has a livid birthmark exactly like a rope burn. Also in the same village, a young boy who said he remembered being stabbed to death bears on his abdomen several congenital marks which are virtually identical to the scars of knife wounds.

In Stevenson's judgment, cases such as these, in which spontaneous recall of a previous life—often with a wealth of verifiable details—is combined with idiosyncratic birthmarks apparently related to the previous experience, represent exceedingly strong evidence that reincarnation is true. (For a detailed description of some of these case histories see Ian Stevenson's book listed in the footnotes, or my book, *Probing the Unexplained*,[6] which contains a long interview with him about his research and its implications.)

What about purported recall of previous lives under hypnosis?

This method—though most parapsychologists believe it has value—is fraught with hazards, chief of which is the unconscious mind's tendency toward dramatic fantasy. What comes out in hypnosis may be, in effect, a dream of the kind of previous existence the subject would like to have lived or believes, correctly or incorrectly, that he did live. Separating fact from fantasy in hypnotic regression is best handled by experts.

One psychologist instructed a number of hypnotized subjects to remember a previous existence, and they did,

[6] Allen Spraggett, *Probing the Unexplained* (New York, World Publishing Co., 1971).

without exception. Some of these accounts were replete with colorful details and seemed convincing. In the waking state all the subjects denied any previous knowledge of the persons they had claimed to be in the past existence or of the details offered as evidence. However, when the psychologist rehypnotized them they were able, in trance, to trace every element in the accounts of previous existence to some normal source—a person they had known in childhood, scenes from novels they had read or movies they had seen years before, and so on.[7]

A psychiatrist, Dr. Harold Rosen, cites a case in which a young man, while hypnotized, began to utter words in a strange language which turned out to be authentic Oscan, a dialect used in Italy in the third century B.C. The subject, still under hypnosis, was able to write what he was saying, and it proved to be an Oscan curse.

Reincarnation? No. Rehypnotized, the subject was able to recall having glanced at an Oscan grammar which happened to by lying open next to him on a library table. The phrases in Oscan had registered in his unconscious mind—though he was not in the least aware of it—and later found expression during the hypnotic state.[8]

However, though instances such as these show the danger of a too-hasty acceptance of purported memories of a past life—especially those produced during hypnosis —they certainly do not prove that *all* such cases are disguised fantasies. Nor do the negative cases totally invalidate hypnotic regression as a method for exploring

[7] E. S. Zolik, "An Experimental Investigation of the Psychodynamic Implications of the Hypnotic 'Previous Existence' Fantasy," *Journal of Clinical Psychology*, Vol. 14 (1958).

[8] Harold Rosen, M.D., *A Scientific Report on "The Search for Bridey Murphy"* (New York, Julian Press, 1956).

purported reincarnational memories. What is needed is care in such regression, and an awareness of the counter-hypotheses, coupled with the quest for hard, verifiable data which would rule out a normal explanation.

One particular hypnotic regression case yielded striking evidence. The case, investigated and vouched for by the Reverend Dr. Leslie Weatherhead, pastor emeritus of London's City Temple and a psychologist of note as well as a clergyman, concerns a Lancashire housewife named Annie Baker who was hypnotized by a Liverpool physician. Under hypnosis, the subject, who had never been to France nor studied French, spoke fluent French and referred to the death of Marie Antoinette as if it had just happened. She gave her own name as Marielle Pacasse and her husband's as Jules. She said she lived on a street in Paris called Rue de St. Pierre near Notre Dame Cathedral. No such street now exists but investigation revealed that there had been a street of that name in the vicinity mentioned by the subject 170 years ago. Also, the name Marielle, though rare nowadays, was popular in the late eighteenth century.

The doctor-hypnotist declared: "Mrs. Baker had not the slightest interest in or knowledge of the French language, the French Revolution, or France itself for that matter." [9]

In a case like this, if it was not an elaborate hoax (which seems very unlikely), there would seem to be only two possible hypotheses: reincarnation, or, again, super-ESP.

However, there is no experimental evidence that a per-

[9] Leslie D. Weatherhead, *The Christian Agnostic* (London, Hodder & Stoughton, 1965).

son, through ESP, can speak a language not consciously
learned, yet in this case the hypnotized subject was said
to speak French fluently; apparently she conversed in it.
This argues strongly against the ESP hypothesis. Moreover, the probability that reincarnation is the correct
hypothesis gathers strength from the other evidence we
have considered which points to rebirth.

If we all have lived past lives, why do we not remember them? Without memory of them, say some critics,
our past lives can do us no good. We cannot learn from
that which we do not remember. The whole moral point
of reincarnation, which is supposed to be growth in spirituality, is lost without remembrance of what we were and,
therefore, why we are what we are.

However, all of us have been shaped by experiences
we had in earliest childhood, none of which, or at least
very few, we remember. Can you recall the interplay
between you and your parents in the first six months of
life? Yet psychoanalysis says that this period is profoundly
important in determining your later personality. Are we
less influenced by those experiences because we cannot
remember them? Or are we, for that reason, *more* influenced by them?

There is another side to the story. Though we do not
have conscious memory of our earliest years we do, apparently, have memory of them. The memory is unconscious.
The experiments of electrical brain stimulation by Wilder
Penfield, in which he evoked distant memories—some of
them beyond normal recall—by touching a person's brain
with an electrode, and the documented cases in which
hypnotic regression has captured what appear to be valid
memories going back to the moment of birth, suggest
that we all carry around inside us a tape recording, as it

were—with not just auditory impressions but all the sense modalities—of everything we have ever experienced. Under certain conditions these memories are accessible.

In the same way, perhaps, etched in the deepest levels of the imponderable mystery which is our human psyche, are memories stretching before birth to other births and deaths beyond. Though we normally have no conscious recall of these far memories they could influence us, as do the unrecalled memories of this life.

Yet I believe that at the deepest level within us, we *do* remember, we do know and understand why we are what we are, we do grasp that everything that happens to us is the result of forces we ourselves unleashed. This profound point within us is perhaps the same as what the mystics mean by the "God within," the spark of the divine fire which lights every man, the "imprisoned splendor."

In truth, then, we know, remember, and understand all at the deepest level; but that awareness only breaks through at rare moments.

In some cases there may be conscious recall, partial or relatively complete, of a previous existence. In children such memories may come spontaneously. The reason why most of Ian Stevenson's cases occur in Asia—though there are many in the West—is that a child in a culture sympathetic to reincarnation does not find his memories being pooh-poohed by parents and other adults. In western countries, when such recall occurs, the child, in the face of parental disapproval, is apt to suppress the memories and as he grows older they fade.

Some people have had apparent recall of past-life memories during psychedelic experiences induced by drugs. A prominent psychiatrist I know experienced under LSD vivid images which he felt came from a previous exist-

ence and which later were independently confirmed by a
medium. Other people have had flashes of past-life memory during meditation or in waking dream states. (Bud-
dhists teach that the way to remember past lives is by
elevating the consciousness through meditation.)

In still other cases, as we've seen, hypnosis is used,
either in a regression or merely with the suggestion that
the person will recall scenes from another time, another
place, which have special meaning for him.

On occasion, a reputable medium gives a life reading
covering a person's purported previous incarnations, or
perhaps reveals only specific "reflections" from the past
life which shed light on his problems in the present.

A medium I know told a friend of mine—a man trained
as an anthropologist but who had strong political ambi-
tions—that the previous life of his which seemed to have
the most bearing on his current one had been spent as a
proconsul in a rather remote and unruly part of the
Roman empire during the twilight of that ancient super-
state. The medium said that he could see the man wearing a helmet with a red plume on it. The red plume, he
added, was a special sign of office.

What the medium did not know was that this man, for
weeks, had been moved by an inexplicable passion to find
a particular kind of authentic Roman helmet. When he
found one he intended to put it on display in his home,
after adding one final touch—a red plume.

Whether the medium here was actually perceiving the
"reflection," as he put it, of a past life or picking up the
man's thoughts by ESP and unconsciously casting them
in the form of a reincarnation fantasy, I do not know.
However, the psychological insights the medium expressed were startlingly accurate and seemed to lay bare

the roots of some problems which had been troubling my friend. Whether reincarnation or ESP, it was a brilliant reading of a man's character and personality, with positive suggestions for self-help.

The mere fact of getting interested in reincarnation seems, in the case of some people, to stimulate a certain amount of past-life recall. These insights may come in dreams, in reveries, while listening to a particular kind of music, by traveling to a particular place, or by merely touching on a certain subject in conversation.

Lawrence Bendit, a British psychiatrist, describes the case of an Englishman who, while visiting Florence, suddenly took ill and ran a high fever. Delirious, he poured out details of a purported previous life in Florence and some of the details were strikingly evidential.[10] Here the stimulation of the local scene plus the altered state of consciousness brought on by the fever seemed to unleash memories hitherto latent.

In another case an elderly couple from the American Midwest, never before out of their native country, stopped at Bombay while on a world cruise. They found themselves having incredible déjà vu ("already seen") experiences around every corner as they strolled through the city's streets. The uncanny sense of familiarity, of having been there before, which both the man and his wife felt, was almost overpowering.

They tested their "memory" by going to a particular spot in the city where they felt a huge house stood with an enormous banyan tree in the front yard. They found neither the house nor the banyan tree. However, a police-

---

[10] L. J. Bendit and Phoebe Payne, *This World and That* (London, Faber & Faber, 1950).

man told them that he remembered his father talking about such a house and such a tree in just that spot. The house, he said, had belonged to a family named Bhan.

The couple were doubly shaken. The name Bhan had always had a peculiar appeal for them, and, in fact, they had given it to their son.[11]

Here, presumably, the locale triggered a chain of recollections previously latent, just as recollections of events in this life may be triggered by something associated with those events.

Such flashes and glimmers recalling past-life do not constitute final proof. But, as part of a picture of converging lines of evidence, they add probability to probability until it amounts to virtual proof. At least, for many individuals.

How strong, how detailed, how precise, is the best evidence for reincarnation?

Consider a recent case investigated by Dr. Ian Stevenson, with a wealth of verified data which propels the mind irresistibly toward the conclusion that reincarnation is a fact of human experience.

The case revolves around a girl named Rajul Shah who was born in Vinchiya, a village in India, on August 14, 1960.[12]

The child started to talk at 12 months and at the age of two-and-a-half began speaking spontaneously of a previous life. She said her name had been "Gita," that she was "small" when she died of a "serious fever." She said

[11] W. C. White, "Cruise Memory," in *Beyond the Five Senses* (New York, Lippincott, 1957).

[12] Ian Stevenson, M. D., "Some New Cases Suggestive of Reincarnation: The Case of Rajul Shah," *The Journal of the American Society for Psychical Research* (July, 1972).

she had lived in a town about a hundred miles away called Junagadh.

The child talked so fluently about her past life, and with such lavish detail, that Rajul's parents and grandparents—she spent some time living with each couple—decided to try to track down this "Gita" and see if she actually had lived, and died. They used a strange (for us) method of tracing the past life. As Jains—members of a Hindu sect which stresses extreme nonviolence and inoffensiveness, even to insects—Rajul's parents believed that the soul cannot exist without a physical body until it has achieved final salvation, and therefore a reincarnated soul must find another body immediately upon the death of the old one. Thus, the child Gita, if she did exist, must have died at the moment Rajul was conceived, so that the soul flew from Gita's into Rajul's body.

Since Rajul was born August 14, 1960, her parents calculated that Gita had died during the last half of October or the first half of November 1959—in other words, at the time of her new body's conception.

Investigation revealed that a child named Gita had indeed died in Junagadh on October 28, 1959, a date exactly in the middle of the period postulated by the Shah family. The name of the dead child's father was given in the municipal records as Gokaldas K. Thacker.

The Thacker family was contacted and arrangements made to take the girl, Rajul, to see them. Rajul, who was five at the time of this first visit, recognized Mr. and Mrs. Thacker as her previous parents and also other members of the family. Her familiarity with the house and with details of the Thackers' life convinced them that she was indeed their dead Gita reborn.

The Thackers belonged to a Hindu sect with different

customs and rites from those of the Jains, the group to which Rajul's family belonged. Some of these differences were among the details which Rajul recalled of her life as Gita.

Ian Stevenson, after careful checking, ruled out any prior contact between the two families as the source of Rajul's information about the Thacker household. The two families, Stevenson was satisfied, had never met before Rajul was taken there.

Here are some of the specific facts—trivial but even more evidential for that—which Rajul cited.

She said Gita's house had two rooms and a kitchen, and a verandah, and was smaller than the house Rajul's grandparents (with whom she stayed for a time) lived in.

She said that her mother, when she was Gita, was Shanta or Kanta. Actually Gita's mother's name was Kanta Ben. (There may have been confusion here since Rajul's grandmother, with whom she lived for various periods, was named Shanta. Rajul, after all, was only five at the time these verifications were made.)

She said Gita's family were Lohanas (members of a subcaste or clan of merchants, Gita's father being a grain merchant).

She said that Gita's father wore dhotis, unlike Rajul's father who wore pajamas. (In India pajamas are cotton trousers usually worn by office workers; dhotis are a kind of long, loose loincloth favored by storekeepers.)

Gita's father, said Rajul, ate from a steel plate while others in the family ate from brass plates. Also, Gita's family had lots of milk in big vessels whereas Rajul's bought it in small quantities in pots.

Gita's family used to eat dinner after dark, while Rajul's ate before sunset.

Gita's parents, said Rajul, used to take her to a temple where the images of the gods "had no clothes," in contrast to the temple she went to as Rajul where the gods' images were all clothed.

As Gita, before she was vaccinated, her parents called her simply "baby," Rajul said. After that they called her Gita.

She died when she was small of a "serious fever," Rajul said. In fact, Gita died, at the age of two years, of measles after five days of sickness and fever.

In addition to these straightforward factual statements, all correct, Rajul recognized, spontaneously and without prompting, various members of Gita's family, and was usually able to call them by name. She showed evident affection when greeting these individuals.

She recognized, for example, Gita's mother, Kanta Ben, and her older sister, Nirmala. She recognized Gita's father and her uncle, as well as her paternal grandmother.

Rajul was also able to identify the particular temple to which Gita was taken by her parents and a candy store (or "sweetshop," as they say in India) which the child had frequented.

All in all, there are some 50 specific units of information, including the instances of recognition of people or places pertaining to the life of the dead Gita, which Rajul mentioned or with which she showed familiarity. This is quite a performance for a five-year-old child. If, as Ian Stevenson is satisfied, normal sources of information must be ruled out, where did Rajul get these facts? Again, the alternatives seem to be reincarnation or ESP.

However, Stevenson points out, not in connection with this case especially but in relation to all the cases he has investigated, that ESP would not account for their behavioral features. The child, that is to say, not only knows facts he has no business knowing but his behavior is consistent with the reincarnation hypothesis. When he comes upon some scene—a building, perhaps, or a street—which was familiar to the former personality, this seems to touch off a stream of new memories, as though by association. This is the way that memory actually works, of course, and Stevenson says he has observed this in case after case. It is as though an adult had returned to the scene of his early childhood and found every sight and sound causing new memories to flood into his mind, only in the reincarnation cases the memories derive from a previous lifetime.

In the case of Rajul, Stevenson suggests that even some of her incorrect statements were the sort of mistakes she might plausibly have made if she were indeed remembering events in her life as Gita, who died at the age of two.

For example, Rajul said that as Gita she had a younger brother. This was incorrect. However, Gita did have a young friend, a boy named Hasmukh, with whom she played a lot and, at two, she might well have considered him a younger brother.

Moreover, says Stevenson, the children in these spontaneous recall cases typically do not experience the recall as sporadic flashes of bits and pieces of information—the way ESP generally seems to function. Rather, they perceive their impressions of the past life as *memories*—as much memories as their recollections of the present life.

When Rajul Singh, in 1970 at the age of 10, was asked if she still remembered her life as Gita, she replied: "Yes, by all means."

Reincarnation harmonizes with the view of survival implied by the evidence in previous chapters. Human life, in this view, exists for the purpose of spiritual growth, the expansion of consciousness in the individual. This process of growth continues after death in a world in which the individual, clothed in a theta body (as discussed earlier), pursues his spiritual development, using the interludes between incarnations as periods for reflection, to distill meaning out of the earth life just ended. Then, when the knowledge has been assimilated, the lessons learned, the mistakes recognized and acknowledged, the self plunges back into this world of time and space to continue the educative process.

And the end of all this?

Who can imagine it, who can conceive it? The absolute perfection which the seers and mystics speak of; our return to the Godhead, infused with the lessons learned in time and space which can be learned in no other way, so that even God himself is enriched; the end of all beginnings, the goal of all striving, the object of all seeking. Who, I ask, can fathom these depths or scale these heights?

All we know is that the mystics, seers, mediums, and prophets who have peered deeper into the mystery assure us that the end is worth the long, drawn-out drama of creation, the weary rounds of the wheel of rebirth, the thirst and hunger of the quest—abundantly, supremely, transcendently worth it all . . .

Index